My Mess
Become Our
Message of
LOVE

My Mess Become Our Message of LOVE

CLAUDIA HENDERSON

ARPress
ILLUMINATING IDEAS
EMPOWERING VOICES

ARPress
45 Dan Road Suite 5
Canton MA 02021

Hotline: 1(888) 821-0229
Fax: 1(508) 545-7580

Ordering Information:
Quantity sales. Special discounts are available on quantity purchases by corporations, associations, and others. For details, contact the publisher at the address above.

Printed in the United States of America.

ISBN-13: Softcover   979-8-89356-389-4
          eBook   979-8-89356-388-7

Library of Congress Control Number: 2024903098

Table Of Contents

Continuation of My Bio:

Share this book with someone you know struggling with a situation. Be bless every day.

One big thanks to Miss Hailey Nelson who help me make this book a reality, she works at Author Reputation Press. To my Lord and my savior Jesus Christ. Thank you, Jesus, for my beautiful daughter Joedian. My mother Vieolda Palmer, my brother Delroy Palmer and to all my family a big thank you to all. My spiritual father pastor T.D Jakes and Trinity Broadcasting Network. To all the ministry I partner, with Pastor Joseph Prince, Daystar Television, Word Channel, Love FM Radio in Jamaica.

Thank you to all who pray for me and supported me in good times and in bad. Jesus' blessing is yours. One more time, thank you to all read and enjoy. Amen

CHAPTER 1:

OUR MESS BECOME OUR MESSAGE OF LOVE

"Weeping may endure for night, but joy come in the morning." - Psalm 30:5

This restoration message of hope was my true my personal trials I have been true in my baby stage, teenage year and adult, when you read this memory, you know Jesus is coming true for you too just be hopeful and have your believe system alive. I was born in the beautiful island of Jamaica next time you plan your vacation go to Jamaica, was born in a life support machine my mother says I have extensive brain damage Jesus heal me when I enter school was a slow learner because of brain damage but Jesus continue to heal us until present, when I was in my teenage was bully, beaten in school and some of my family verbally and physical abuse me, but is very important Jesus never let me go true the trial he was with me every step of the way. I am writing this book from 2019 because Jesus needs me to write it, never plan on writing this book but I was in 3 days prayer and fasting when Jesus says get your book and pen and start write that 2019 of the easter holiday yes, I start write. I am inspired by Jesus and the Holy Spirit to preach, pray, to worship and do the things of God and write this timely book that the best way to be effective in ministry and see personal life have victory.

Growing up as kids I see my mother and father struggle to simple provide food, cloth and pay bill but Jesus was aways in our family we pray as family, go to the house of God as a family because we pray always as family I see Jesus miracle power multiple in our own family from 1 bedroom with lot children to owning our own house consist of

4 bedroom, 3 bathroom and lot more room, my father was promoted from A COMMON labor to second in charge of the company my mother was the most sort after business women, and most of my family brother and sister go back to school and simple get an education, But most important we all continue to serve Jesus until present, when Jesus restore your life don't turn your back on him But keep serving Jesus until he come don't let money, fame, relationship or peer pressure let us lose out on God you will live to regret it.

I remember for year when I live on my own, I was straying from Jesus going with friends to party, club, doing thing Jesus never please of my lifestyle, Jesus never leaves even in those time of recklessness he starts to show me dream I get when he take to a church in Spanish town, Jamaica in the dream he take me to a Church when I arrive at the church the church gate lock and I stand outside crying saying Jesus let me in everyone in the Church have on white grown and Jesus himself came before me and say "you are cast out repent Claudia" after Jesus spoke to me every one in the church fly straight up to heaven Jesus lead the march and I Claudia was crying like a baby when I wake up out the dream I was crying kneeling down praying to God to save my thirst soul thank Jesus for 25 year he save me and fill me with the Holy spirit. If you are reading this timely book let Jesus save your soul and fill you with the Holy. St. John 3:16 say for God so love the world that he gave his only begotten son, if you believe in Jesus, you will not perish but have everlasting life now is the right time we are at the end of the world.

When I was writing my book some many set back from 2019 to 2020 was distracted, my new laptop breaks down, I went for a walk in my neighborhood was nob and rob end up in the hospital here in Florida I got rob in august of 2020, but I pray to Jesus to help me finish my book so many people especially going true trying time this message can be encourage them. 2019 I end up with a severe back pain I was going to the emergency room, but I remember Jesus is my healer and I pray the Holy Spirit pray at home and use my healing Olive Oil with my prayer shawl the next morning as believe and expected Jesus heal all my back pain. We talk about our mess become our message of love,

Jesus is waiting to help you only believe all things are possible when we believe Jesus is not partially, I am confident he will do it for you anywhere in the world you are whether in the prison, jail, at home, at work, flying walking our distance and location does not matter just faith believing for your miracle. We must all have a relationship with Jesus and have the Holy Spirit to really tap in the supernatural realm of God there are two spirit the satanic spirit and the Jesus spirit so be careful which spirit you receive relationship will tell you the right holy word, the right spirit. In this 20th century we got to be careful of false teacher, false preacher how to know if they are false pray to Jesus to show you where to worship, pray about if the preacher if of God or not.

Jesus our savior, our High Priest, our soon coming king went true a lot of mess too not because he was the Son of God, he goes true the trial just like us born in a stable the lowest place on earth where only animal to live that where Jesus was born, King Herod plan was to destroy Jesus when he was born because he knows Jesus' purpose on earth to save human kind from sin but Herald thought Jesus was coming to take over his earthly throne so he was intimated Jesus Mother Mary and Joseph have to run to Egypt with baby Jesus to avoid hurt. The angel of God tells Mary she can come back to Bethlehem because the enemy Herod die.

Matthew 2:13 and when they departed behold the angel of the Lord appear to Joseph in a dream saying arise and take the young child Jesus and his mother and flee into Egypt be there until I bring thee word for Herod will seek to destroy the baby. When Jesus start is earthly ministry at 30 years old some of is same Jewish people rejected saying he was not the promise messiah because of where he was from, the Master was rejected talk about, abuse just like us here on earth even though they see the miracles, the good things he does some of them never believe on Jesus, they oppose him daily instead of embracing him. You see Jesus go true what we been true rejection, abandonment, bet way so if you are a sole out Christian that have the character of Jesus you will go true what our Master been true, stop beat up on yourself saying why me Jesus? Jesus lives a perfect life on earth no sin whatever compassionate, sharing, giving, holy and pure yet is enemies still put him true hell. They put him in jail, falsely accuse him, beat him and kill him on that ragged old cross but guess what? Jesus never fight back he was humble, voiceless to his untimely dead.

So, keep in the word of God, be a doer of God word, stay pray up daily, keep focus and be and the alert, be around spirit fill believer that connection is in Jesus Godly mentor that can be there for you and bring you to God place of Honor. Nobody perfect but Jesus but when you read God word, pray and praise Jesus everyday perfection is yours, example physical you got to eat food and drink water every day to nourish your body, if you don't take care of your house or car it will mash up it is same with your spiritual life is must you have to pray, read the bible and worship everyday else the devil will take over your life period., don't let him steal and destroy your life that's why Jesus came to give you a better life' the way for many people all over the world to receive Jesus salvation receive Jesus in your heart and believe serve him. John is one that baptize Jesus, John was preaching saying repent because the kingdom is at hand, that was the perfect work of God but the enemies never thing so they cut of the apostle head because he preaches holiness. John mess became is message of salvation we will see john in heaven your sickness, poverty will soon come to an end stop worry and start have faith in God it doesn't matter what you are going true believe there is an alive Jesus will rescue us all.

King David was chosen of God to be Israel King but when the Prophet Samuel go an anoint David is own family reject him because he was cast out of the family, but God was looking at the job David have, or the color of David skin. David was just a Shepherd boy taking care of his father sheep some people look down on that Job title Jesus was looking at David heart and obedient that why God choose David because the present King Saul fail to obey God. David Mess start at home, then he have to face the giant goliath this giant was fighting from his youth nobody every beat him in Israel the army of Israel was afraid of him because of his height and statue but when David saw goliath David say tomorrow this time I will defeat you say God., the giant laugh at David but David have the Holy Spirit, and Jesus to defend him big time yes David win the Big giant be not afraid face your mess knowing Jesus is fighting your battle right now no more enemies, no more lack, no more loneliness, no more evil Jesus fight for David he still fighting for you right in 2020 and beyond believe. Apostle David goes to fight and win all the gangs the devil set up against him because God was with David and Jesus is with us, we are is chosen people black, white, rich or poor. Amen

Father Abraham wife Sarah and Prophetess Ann in the bible could not have kids they were barren women of God, but they pray to Jesus never give up in their old age over 90-year-old finally God open their womb and they have children when al reproductive organs close down. Even if you are going true spiritual or physical bareness believe the blood of Jesus is breaking our bareness right now, God kingdom operate in faith, believe and receive.

Joseph in the bible was a messes true story from a favor son of his mother and father Jacob to be envy by his own brother because he tells them the dream God show him of increase and promotion Jesus speak to us in dream read about dream in Daniel. So is bother conspire against joseph literally throw in the pit to die, God send the Egyptian to get out of the pit of hell was raise in one richest family in Egypt because the favor of God was on Joseph, Pharoah wife tell lie on Joseph say he try to rape her which was a lie joseph end up spent some time in prison for something he never does some of you can relate to joseph unfortunate story. But Joseph finds with the ruler of Egypt Pharoah because only joseph could interpret his dream God gave him from the pit to prison Guest what Jesus promote joseph to second in charge of Egypt because the favor of God was on his life from birth true to his adult life. Jesus is doing the same for all of us not because we going true trial that God don't love us yes, he does love us we all as Christian as to go true something when you sold out to God.

Some many restoration story I read from I am writing this book in 2019 present 2020 healing, deliverance, financial increase having receive family husband, wife etc. share some brief resurrection testimony: a poor man from Tanzanian Africa having A lot of Children go hunting a God allow him to find a GEM Stone this stone is the one that make Diamond and gold and silver the government of Africa give him 7.0 billion dollar for the gem stone equivalent US$300 million from a poor man to one of the richest man in the world. Right here in the US in early part of the year 2020 this man buys the lotto for $2 us right multi-millionaire that how Jesus blesses when he chooses God is a mysterious God nobody can program God, he says the wealth of the wicked lay on the just meaning lotto money, stealing money when Jesus gives us pray for those money and spend it to do Jesus' work here on earth and help the poor and needy, that why he gives in the first place. Testimony of Shirley Chisholm is resurrection story become the first Black women elected to the United States congress in 1968 when America was racial segregated you hardly see black elected to us congress that was great and faith of her.

This Muslim family never believe in Jesus their religion was Aliha but something miraculous happen in their family some of the family member was drug and alcoholic to top it off their mother has cancer Jesus' step in and heal their family, right now all family member is serving Jesus and fill with the Holy Spirit.

So many people all over the world get heal of Corona virus, save, all kind of sickness, get miracle money, see love ones come home to their family that who Jesus is after the trial there come the victory in our life. Shout thank you Jesus, glory, halleluiah just pause a little and praise Jesus even if you don't get a miracle start thanking Jesus for your miracle.

2 young ladies in the bible name ruth and ester they were just regular people like all of us ester was taken away from Israel to Babylon her mother and father die in exile or her uncle medical was left she was really out of it only God could give her miracle to bring and her uncle to life, they come to India Ethiopia just searching was a better life just like some of us looking for a better life in different part of the world is the same thing. But God allow ester to find favor with the richest man in that region the King Ahasuerus guess what? The King marries to the rejected ester because of the favor Jesus have for her. Same with ruth was from a different county name Moabites but because of Nahum going to that country because there was famine in Israel so ruth end up marrying to Nahum son but the son die and Nahum was leaving

the Moabites country ruth agree to follow Nahum thank Jesus she did when ruth arrive in Israel she met one of the most influential man in Israel name Boaz own all the land and field ruth start work with Boaz and finally became Boaz wife go back to Jesus favor God gave us beauty for ashes he gave us something for nothing. Keep your dream alive don't quit, don't give him, don't sell yourself out for money and fame you will live to regret it. Some many Christians sell out their ministry for money and fame now they are sorry they did Jesus will give you more than what the world offer you amen read it old testimony ruth and ether they both are separate book the really hopeful story.

For our Mess to change we have to be obedient to what Jesus tell us to do it sometimes it may not make sense in naturally but when we obey Jesus later down the road you see great reward. Jesus 12 apostle was working when Jesus goes to them say leave your fishing trade, leave your nursing profession, leave your cleaning jobs, leave your husband or wife, leave your business etc. and follow me is either you obey and loose the blessing of Jesus just simple obedient. Jesus disciple never loose nothing only 1 judas kill himself for selling out Jesus Peter was forgiven and receive back in fold was even be the Head of 11 Apostle. As believer when you sin against God just know when you come humble and repent of all your sin Jesus will forgive you but stop sinning everyday try to pray be in relationship daily so we sin less that really the solution for sin if you don't have a relation with Jesus start now in this 2020 stay away from religion those pharisee and scribes call themselves Christian but was not doing what God tell them to do their works was evil and judgmental, they oppose Jesus when he was here on earth instead of support him and embrace him it was so sad to see our own believers, our own family, our own co-worker and friend regret us and talk about us not just Jesus but us nowadays 20th Christian. Learn the game of forgiveness big time and move on that how Jesus bless flow true simple obey and forgive. I have to learn to forgive all who hurt me including those who are close to me including family, friends, Christian and close friends you do the same.

Because we please Jesus our heart is clean, your attitude is good, our action is good we see he work for us every day, result is: good health, financial increase, favor increase in every area of our life. Dr, Creflo Dollar say is not just money alone but we must rich in faith, rich in God rich how we communicate with each other that so true. Joyce Meyer says enjoy everyday life not having party everyday but simply go out with friends, family for just drinking, to the beach sometime just being alone reading a good book, watching a good movie, cooking a good dinner just do something you like. Jesus our Leader was single, Apostle Paul was single that write most of the New Testament in the bible it never bothers them they enjoy their life on earth. Don't let people initiate you because you are single or you are a widow gave us beauty for ashes he gave us something for nothing. Keep your dream alive don't quit, don't give him, don't sell yourself out for money and fame you will live to regret it. Some many Christians sell out their ministry for money and fame now they are sorry they did Jesus will give you more than what the world offer you amen read it old testimony ruth and ether they both are separate book the really hopeful story.

For our Mess to change we have to be obedient to what Jesus tell us to do it sometimes it may not make sense in naturally but when we obey Jesus later down the road you see great reward. Jesus 12 apostle was working when Jesus goes to them say leave your fishing trade, leave your nursing profession, leave your cleaning jobs, leave your husband or wife, leave your business etc. and follow me is either you obey and loose the blessing of Jesus just simple obedient. Jesus disciple never loose nothing only 1 judas kill himself for selling out Jesus Peter was forgiven and receive back in fold was even be the Head of 11 Apostle. As believer when you sin against God just know when you come humble and repent of all your sin Jesus will forgive you but stop sinning everyday try to pray be in relationship daily so we sin less that really the solution for sin if you don't have a relation with Jesus start now in this 2020 stay away from religion those pharisee and scribes call themselves Christian but was not doing what God tell them to do their works was evil and judgmental, they oppose Jesus when he was here on earth instead of support him and embrace him it was so sad to see our own believers, our own family, our own co-worker and friend regret us and talk about us not just Jesus but us nowadays 20th Christian. Learn the game of forgiveness big time and move on that how Jesus bless flow true simple obey and forgive. I have to learn to forgive all who hurt me including those who are close to me including family, friends, Christian and close friends you do the same.

Because we please Jesus our heart is clean, your attitude is good, our action is good we see he work for us every day, result is: good health, financial increase, favor increase in every area of our life. Dr, Creflo Dollar say is not just money alone but we must rich in faith, rich in God rich how we communicate with each other that so true. Joyce Meyer says enjoy everyday life not having party everyday but simply go out with friends, family for just drinking, to the beach sometime just being alone reading a good book, watching a good movie, cooking a good dinner just do something you like. Jesus our Leader was single, Apostle Paul was single that write most of the New Testament in the bible it never bothers them they enjoy their life on earth. Don't let people initiate you because you are single or you are a widow get with roommate, friends and family and good believer to fellowship. You don't have to wait for a husband and a wife to enjoy your life the devil is liar go out and enjoy yourself okay.

When Jesus wants to use us do great think, we go true great trial than an ordinary person Apostle Moses was hide for 3 months of his life because those days they ruler want to kill because male babies, Moses' mother hide him because he was a proper child God have big plan for Moses' adult life, he ended up God use to go back in Egypt to free the children of Israel out wicked pharaoh hand. Me Claudia being true hell too growing up physical abuse, rejected, abandon, car accident, rob until present Jesus is still with me every step of the way. So, my friend it does matter what you are going thru don't give up hold on tell Jesus rescue us, we you give up the devil win and your loss and sorry you make that choice. I remember many years ago I was suicidal because of problems and hopelessness because I never know Jesus was in my everyday life Hope of God came in my heart thank you Jesus, he rescues us in time. Tell your testimony so other people can be rescue too and save from there despair, but don't go around and gossip other when you can pray for them and encourage them in God word okay.

The world we are living in full of problems rich, poor, black and white you are not alone.

As I write this long awaiting book right Christian from all over the world, we celebrate The Day of Atonement the Jews call it Yom Kippur supposed to be the holiest day of the year meaning asking Jesus to forgive us of our sin we committed murder, fornication, lying, stealing, gossiping evil we need to stop doing wrong things and please Jesus. Right now, in 2020 we are seeing God wrath pour out earthquake, hurricane, corona virus, plane cash, lot of people dying from various cause. When God take the children of Israel out of bondage he gives them angel food milk, honey their life was far better than when they were in Egypt, but they go ahead and still sin against God worship false God, complain against God unthankful is wrath pour on them some die and some suffer bitterly. When Jesus blesses and take you out of grave situation don't go back to where he takes you from, else you will live to regret it. This Christian journey is easy when you make it up in your heart and mind I will live for Jesus as long as you keep Jesus in your heart every day and take out things you heart that wore you out and keep you stress and depress like unlikeness, bitterness, envy and war learn to forgive and forget let Jesus deal with all your worry when you pray leave everything on the altar, that Jesus take everything to God in prayer not some stuff all our concern and pain. Enjoy Jesus abundant life of peace, love and joy he gave everyone because of his sacrifice on the ragged cross start enjoying God live even if you live alone, don't have no job, sick make up in your mind I am still enjoying my life. The Mess you are going true is temporarily not permanent so road in America have tunnel and train track when we are driving it so dark and dusty but at end, we see sunshine and light. Spiritual, it does matter the pain and struggle hold on tell your change come. Pastor Marvin Wigans Singer Cede wigans was diagnose with Covid 19 early in 2020 Jesus miraculous heal him, Pastor Percy Spencer of Virginia U.S.A. was also infected with same virus Pastor never stop pray and worship on that hospital bed of course Jesus heals him. Pastor Phillip Dunn was blind for 14 year the Doctor diagnose him with Macular degeneration with cause damage to sharp central vision, pastor pray and worship faith believing he was completely healing is vision is very perfect, only believe all thing are possible when we believe Jesus. Jesus still do miracle go for your miracle the women in bible have blood condition for 13 year nonstop bleeding she believe Jesus I was heal, rich and powerful Naaman was full of leper and Jesus heal him, the king daughter Jesus raise from the dead and lazes was raise for the dead The Doctor pronounce Lazarus his family bury him in the tomb he was not in the marge he was already bury, but Jesus miraculous heal Lazarus we still talking our mess is going be what Jesus need for our message keep your hope alive resurrection time raise up and face our challenge don't run from it over come all battles. Most of Jesus miracle find in Matthew, Mark, Luke and John Read all these book day by day with the holy spirit and Jesus to help you understand the word better.

I remember when Jesus calls me to Preach his word, I never hesitate I take up is call to lead people to God, I was wavering and stubborn when he was calling me to repentance thank Jesus, I receive the best gift any human being would every need in their life the gift of salvation. Second call was to be his ministry, his mouth and hand her on earth thank Jesus I never hesitate I was obedient to do it right away with rejoicing and glad he chooses me as his ambassador here on earth. So far 25 years from Jamaica I still preaching until present 2020, go to England, Canada preach right here in the USA Florida where I reside, Atlanta, Louisiana Mississippi, Virginia, Texas, New York and California and Jesus still sending in more country all over the world if anyone out there need to come and spread Jesus good news of his peace, love and salvation feel free to contact us at 754 368 9454 for more information. This ministry is a Holy Spirit, relationship style ministry not religion or occultic ministry let people know before you come and pray to Jesus before you take this very important call. God send Jesus here on earth to let people know who he really his because a lot false preacher falsifying Jesus Church he pay his life for this church our high priest any believer out there preaching false doctrine right now stop and do it Jesus way not your way or man ways, Saul was one of the false apostle going around persecuting Christian and abusing them and claim in was a Christian, but when Jesus met on the way his life change immediately transformation from false apostle to Jesus chosen vessel even his name God change from demonic Saul to Apostle Paul he is one write most of New Testament, let Jesus transform and restore our life to brand new. Then impossible Jesus super natural unipotent, ominous program Jesus' way is not our way and his thought are not our thought., Jesus takes a murderer and turn him into a Man of God, the prostitute he turns into wife, cheater and sneaker and robber into Great man of God make him be the nation of Israel which bring the 12 tribe of Israel that Jacob, Moses and Gomer. The women were giving her testimony of Facebook she was former prostitute and have a lot of abortion Doctor literally take her womb out because of many abortions the doctor tell her she cannot have children any more. One day she accepts Jesus as lord and savior guess what God gave her a Husband and she pray for Jesus to heal her ovaries for her to have baby thank Jesus her husband make love to her and Jesus create new Ovaries and she give birth to 3 baby girl the impossible Jesus. That why God send Jesus is son for those who are not save meaning the prostitute, dunkers, the thief Jesus never came for the rightness indeed some of the believer oppose him and conspire against him believe it is own people some of you people can relate to Jesus's story I can personally relate to Jesus' story because most time is my own people the devil use to fight against me big time. But always pray up, be on the alert watch Jesus will fight our battle every time we have a trial.

I try my best to make this book short and brief but precise to reader may get the main point of resurrection and RESTORATION Finally your Mess what Jesus want to turn your situation into diamond and gold be patients all my reader the miracle you waiting for so long his now in 2020. Read 1 & 2 Samuel, read genesis read ruth and Esther all in the Holy Bible, read job and Psalm no Apostle try like Job he loss everything even is family but job never stop believing until God restore everything to him in greater style and job get brand new family too. Read Mathew, Mark, Luke and John. So much God good word in the Holy bible to keep you possible and encourage every single day all day THE HOLY BIBLE is good road map to lead us to our destination final stop is paradise heaven where there is no war, no hate. Turn with me to the chapter on prayer.

CHAPTER 2:

WORSHIP AND PRAISE

"O let sing to the lord a new holy spirit song all nations bless is name Jehovah God shew forth his salvation every day." - Psalm 96:1 & 2

Now all my reader so far you come with me to the end of this God send book: worship is very important to God and his son Jesus, because it was worship and honor to God cause the fall of lucifer you see the devil was the director of music in heaven he first see how all the angel was praising and worshipping our father God, but instead of help celebrate God he was so jealous and envy of the one that create him God that he start fighting against God and he go further want to take charge of the throne of God you better believe it. Just like you own a house and some jealous family member or friend want to take it over, that how the bad devil wants to take charge of what is not is because of God honor and worship, but the warrior angel Michael lead the gang of angel and war back with the devil and his gang and Michael won but the victory continue they finish him off put him down here on earth the bible say he fall like the star falling and he came with wrath in his heart and mouth. Don't let the devil deceive you, from day one the devil is defeat when Moses free the slave in Egypt we won, when we worship and live holy, we won, when you resist the devil we won, when you reject and abandon and ignore the devil we won, when you evict the devil we won, the song says no more for the devil sing by Maria providence she is worship get her song I personally play her song every day.

In this present world we are living in what connect people is God Jesus, music, love and peace, good word that what connect people all over the world. I happen to travel to England to do mission when I was there a president of the USA was there and I was shock to see the whole England come out to tell him you are not welcome in my country. Be careful what in your heart, what you represent and stand for most important what come out of your mouth, how you behave because people are watching you and most important Jesus is watching you your children watch too children live what they see before them, they are the one that going to take our place my friends. Do you know some people they are rude and always waring they have the devil personality and character they lie, they cheat, they always gossiping and talking bad thing you don't want to be around those people unless you are like them? I personal use to live with these families when I leave Jamaica and come to live in the USA, they were Christian but their action speak differently they war like a sinner I have to leave their home and guess where I ending living in my car that where peace was. You see some wealthy people not enjoying their life because of who is around them it can be their families, friend and coworker, money cannot make you happy only Jesus can with his love in you can keep you happy. So be careful who is around you and your circle, my advice let Jesus choose all who must be around you including your wife and husband and friends and family's God in is mighty power from beginning created the world for us to enjoy in love, peace and joy all he is asking us serve him and worship him every day celebrate him with honor we are taking praise and worship. You have to know the process leading up to know him in all his glory my brother and sister. I hear this preacher say I was reading his book Mr. Andrew Womack he says there was a big bill he has to pay for the house of God but as old fashion preacher he applies Jesus and he simple start to worship God and from nowhere someone call his phone and give some well needed money, so he pays the bill and have left over paint God good: pause a little stop and worship Jesus' shout with joy of praise. The song says *it amazing what praise can do hallelujah* this is a working book read absorb it like reading the bible and sometime you have to stop and start thank Jesus and worship apply the same rule with this best seller as write I stop too and worship and pray so more inspiration can flow to write. When God was building the earth, he stops and worship that he created the earth perfectly and he finish it we as believers not going to finish praise God until Jesus come even when they come is more praise this the only work that is not will finish everything will finish but the praise and worship will not finish it must be in your heart even sleeping, in the shower anywhere you are is in your heart. You see king David before he was a king and he use to take care of his father sheep he in the mountain in his heart he was worship so when God call him, he come with experience fully loaded to continue worship that make him the greatest worshipper as shepherd boy and a promoted king the greatest and best king we have seen until today. David restores the worship to a higher dimension like Michael Jackson the greater entertainer of all time, bob Marley, Dennis brown, Whitney Houston I hear Whitney's brother say when she was little, she uses the mop and go on the high stair in her house pretending it was a mike and singing before the world know her like king David.

This best book I read on worship is pastor rick warren book name *The Purpose Driven Life* all worshipper, singer, members, choir member and director must get this book simple these are resources we need to read with the bible. We all must strive to grow in God not just at your work place or your business and your personal life, but most importantly grow in God so the devil cannot take charge of you and demonic spirit. We getting deep I am in prayer and fasting writing this book so it easy for me to get Jesus in all is glory amen. All happiness, all blessing, all holiness all good gift where it come from the root *God* so when you work, serve Jesus, run your business or anything you do it is prosperous not because of you but because of one that give favor *Jesus*. Why not honor give him the credit just like these actor and actress when they get there award only few gives Jesus the credit, they give first the producer and those who they work with nothing wrong with that but first give honor to God don't eat God glory else you are in big trouble with him. I was watching so old tape of singer and my friend Whitney Houston is one of my favorite singers when I she was receiving her award, she first gives honor to God because of course she starts sing in her church in new jersey she was super famous until present she is the voice until present. I am calling on all who Jesus give talent and gift start use you God given gift and talent and don't hide it use for the upliftment of God glory if you are going to church and they don't want you do what God call you to do, go and talk to the pastor if he doesn't want you to participate leave and ask Jesus where to go most great singer and dancer come from the church okay. I was at a church right here in Florida USA but I realize that the pastor never even wants us to testify or do nothing, first I go and talk to him couple time settle it with them and nothing happen I leave say God and guess what? From I leave I am all over the world preaching. So, be careful where you go worship some of this pastor is simple not of God, they not even hearing from God, that why they treat God children like trash but move on and forgive them release them to Jesus but first settle it with them before you leave. For example, you have a dispute with your boss you have to settle it before you go don't it. That why from couple year I see a pastor, members losing your faith because they want to do it their way and not God way i go to a temple here in Florida and I have to disgrace the pastor before the congregation that not what i plan but the pastor was like a gang leader so before the people, i treat him like a criminal he was so ashamed of himself that God say do it. You see when you read the holy bible and have the spirit of God with your worship you see spiritual that how you know who is real and who is false you will not know in the flesh, we as believers call it spirit of discernment.

I lady invite me to her temple couple year when I go God spirit in me was twisted trouble watch this principle, I never ask nobody what going on at the church not even the lady that invite me I ask Jesus when I come home in my prayer room I showing people we serve a live God not even 2 week Jesus take me in a dream and show me the same pastor in question on the stage with a gun that what twist my spirit at first when I go there. The flesh could not tell me I never gossip with nobody but I ask the one that see and know the heart of all people. So as believe be careful who you ask God business because some of these Christian just not connected to God like the scribes and pharisee never know Jesus all they know is religion and get some money it bad. Ministry is serious business no playing around and playing church if you are doing it stop and repent and start doing it God way not your way. Everything starts with God the church, the work, governmental system, family system and all system okay so if we can" t represent Jesus on this earth we fail in our personal and public life because we fail to put him first. When Jesus calls me, it was at my work place okay that telling me I have to continue work but for him this work never finishes the only thing is different it preaching to people helping and empowering people on deeper level so if you want to come and help us as preaching, prayer warrior come abroad call 754 368 9454. This lady in new jersey quit his job and travelling the world so if God call you come, I leave my job and preaching all over the world I love it I am fulfill when people can receive Jesus because they hear it from my mouth, I was sitting in temple when they were going to baptize people the same day and this young lady say is me she saw in a park in lot and I tell her about Jesus I was one of the proudest person in that temple because I preach to someone and she accepted Jesus as lord and savior. I want to know when I leave this earth, I know that someone was bless because I open wide my mouth and preach Jesus and I know that someone reading this book will be save to and be encourage and deliver that my purpose Jesus have me to do here on earth. Even recently I was dreaming I was on stage preaching in January 2022 when I wake, I remember some of what I was preaching and I journal it, I see these dream more than one time lot of time Jesus confirm with me that what I should be doing. So, all that say they are working in the kingdom of God let the master Jesus confirm with you what you should be doing, if the pastor hearing from God they will tell and Jesus himself will let you know. Look at Joyce Meyer the world know who Joyce is famous tele evangelist she was with a ministry but God himself get her and give her is own ministry and so far so good sister Juanita Bynum was with a ministry too and God give her is own ministry so far she all over the world preaching, I Claudia Henderson was with a ministry I mention early and God take me and give me is ministry so far so good I am all over the world preaching to God be the glory and I know some of my reader God take you from somewhere and give you your own ministry put in you name…and say God I thank. God choose not us he is the master of all just do and obey be humble and learn his way of doing things and do it we need to come in unit forget about ourselves concentrate on him keep focus and worship him, it was 2 sisters when

Jesus come in their home to speak God words but one of the sister sit at Jesus feet and get every word the other sister was busy doing work, Mary that sat at Jesus feet get all and was full, be like Mary all my reader turn of the radio, television, your phone and listen Jesus speak to you after you worship and pray, it a 2 way conversation lean on him.

We need people like Mary when I was going to school, I use to like talk that sometime the teacher says Claudia go outside and I was punish for talking too much, but talking to much was not a bad idea but don't talk when someone talking to you when they finish tell you talk that what Jesus was saying in Mary and martyr situation the big word *listen*. Look at this Jesus use the talking and say go preach my word use the talking and write a book use the talking and encourage someone okay. Don't use the talking and gossip and just like to talk and put yourself in trouble and lie you don't have nothing to say keep your tongue between your teeth shut your mouth. We have lot of talk show on radio and television when I watch and listen some of them some of the topic really good some is going to deep in people business, so be careful what you listen and watch you and your family. We must put border to who we really are no when to stop and no when to go you don't go around and beg respect earn it my friends, sometime people may not like you but the life you live they don't have a choice but to respect you.

So we are worshipping Jesus are we and praising him for everything good and bad time in season and out of season be the weapon of your worship king David was the weapon of his worship, that how he won even when his own son come against him to destroy him David weapon was worship and praise this a chance to praise God but your heart must be saying what your word says I love read encouraging book with my bible that how you grow feed your spiritual soul and spirit just like you eat physical food every day and water, pastor john gray write a book on the heart name *win from within* please read these resource it help us grow in God, heart worship not lip service Jesus need real people he can rely on like how our children and boss reply on us to work, Jesus is relying on us the same way please don't let him down believers. When the time come, we got to show what we have we are in the ring of war come out and be victorious be the ever-burning light that people want to be around us. All who God chose to work for him is a worshipper, prayer warrior, preacher, a prophets but bottom line they worship God, now Jacob have two wife but he love one more than the other so the one that he despite give him the tribe of Israel when she have the 7 of the children God give that one name Judah-meaning praise she say now will I praise God. Genesis 29:35 we are living in the last day don't waste anytime use your precious time and praise the lord, preach his word do sometime for God when the children of Israel get out of bondage they start to worship and thank Jesus for their release there song was *they right hand o lord is become glorious in power thy right hand o lord dash in pieces our enemy and in the greatness of thine excellency thou overthrown our enemies* read that song in exodus 15 especially all the hard core worshipper. I see God getting ready to bless you before your haters and exalt you and promote you, the enemies will surrender receive this prophetic word it for you, you being task around, rejected but don't worry your pain is over rejoice I say rejoice it over.

For years growing up I was beaten, abuse, bully in school, rejected and lost my self-esteem could not find my proper self, some people tell me I was ugly, but when I found Jesus as my lord and savior, he tells me I am queen I am beautifully and wonderfully made, then the real people start tell how beautifully I was when I look in the mirror, I see how beautiful I was for sure. I know some of my reader can relate to my and other people story black or white you are God king and queen beauty is from the heart not the outside appearance. Prophetess continue to celebrate their freedom she takes the children of Israel after their release and let them in a time of worship and praise they bring their timbrel and dance before Jesus, so we can worship for something God done in your life heal your body, set you free from prison, led you through the valley of dead and destruction and block you from our enemies. I was sitting in my car resting I hear the voice of Jesus say *the stone have been roll away* it means we are free bless his holy name he rolls it away all my friends., there is old fashion singer name sister Scully sing this song *he rolls the sea away* these are good worship song to continue sing in churches, every situation has song or scripture to compliment what you are going through. Just like every man have wife out there and all women have a husband don't worry God will find them for you in due time just wait on Jesus, these are quality word for your everyday knowledge. Stop feed on garbage like eating junk food that let you sick feed on the undeleting word of God good report, word of good nutrients that when you read and digest this word you always need more and want to tell everyone read God word just like you read the newspaper. I love to read the holy bible it gives me a good report and a true one of myself it will do the same for you, so spent time and read the bible and pray with your worship. So after the children of Israel pass over the different country they have a celebration jubilee praise in the day of atonement we shall sound the trumpet throughout the world and pull down everything the devil put on you worship get it of no more doing evil, and we shall get back our possession with our family they are coming believe the missing coming home, when I was writing this book a friend in Canada can't find her son let pray, he is coming home believe Jesus will restore everything the enemies stole from us and more. The bible says after king Jehoshua worship and won the enemies God tell them take the enemies silver and gold it your so jubilee is now read Leviticus 25:9 to 13. It does not matter how severe the situation is don't stop believing even if the doctor pronounces you dead, he can bring you back to life Jesus is resurrection and the life believe.

Remember giving his worshipping God so we must give her praise, give our money, give our service first unto God and then chose where you want to give, so now you know that giving is worshipping give cheerfully and gladly love to give and share. Number 3:48 and 49 thou shall give the money wherewith the odd number of them to be redeemed unto Aaron and his sons, and Moses took the redemption money of them that was over and above them that were redeemed by the Levites, so I prove in the word of God that giving is a must. God gave his son Jesus to save us from sin and shame that giving not just money but he gave us family and friends and people to enjoy. Give your tithes and offering Moses say the blessing *the lord bless you and keep thee the lord make his face shine upon thee and be gracious unto thee, the lord lifts up his countenance upon thee and give us peace. And they shall put thy name upon the children and I God will continue to bless them* that certify blessing from Jesus it more blesses to give than to receive make it easy to give and looking different ways of giving sometime take the bus or drive your car and bring some clothes or food and bless someone and is perfect opportunity to share Jesus word, you not begging them to listen but leave everything in Jesus hand, he says after you finish your part God will finish his part. Your blessing the lord give to you and your family will not reverse that blessing is seal unto God come so go enjoy that blessing and more to come our father is Abraham the blessing himself from day one until his dead at 100-year-old he lives a bless life never suffer so we not going to suffer.

I read out your blessing for all to see Deuteronomy 28 *it shall come to pass that these blessing is for you if you keep God commandment and teach them to your family and who you chose to get them, these blessing is under condition if you obey God law and statute: we will bless in the field, bless in our body and bless when you cultivate, bless that when the enemies see you coming the shall flew, all your store house will be full your kitchen cover will be full that you have to give your neighbors. The lord will establish us a holy people unto himself anywhere you go my brother and sister you are bless please read all of Deuteronomy 28 and read the whole bible so you see you are in the will of God when you serve him in spirit and truth. You see you don't know because you don't take time and read the word is not just word of mouth you must have to read the word of God okay. Keep therefore the word of his covenant and do them that we may prosper in all you do we are a chosen generation a royal priesthood and a holy nation I am honor to be chosen of God are you honor to call son and daughter? Now the worship that torn down patrician in our life Jericho wall represent sin and disgrace that what we don't want but Joshua was facing the enemies from all over but guess what get him out praise and worship he let the worshipper with harp, trumpet, horn so they position them self to play the instrument and sing unto the lord with a voice of triumphant, they go 7 time but the last time the enemies was indeed defeated not by gun and knife but with sound of worship and praise. Read Joshua 6:1 to 27. It means that sometime you dealing with some situation you pray, you sing, your pastor and members pray nothing happen you still sick, you try get a job nobody want to employ you, but bottom line don't give up keep believing that it will happen one day it finally happen amen. Before Joshua and his worship team get the victory they have to go 7 time not one time but 7 day and they finally get the victory start worship and stop talk defeat Jesus pay it on the rugged old cross for me and you, blood run, he fell on the ground so many time, he was thirsty and, bruise and condemned by the mob, you may be going true pain and sorrow but don't give up press on but it was finally victory at last martin Luther king says free at last so pause and worship…

Moses's God let use a rod, but Joshua God allows to use a spear when they were passing over the different land that spear clear the way for them to go through, just like we use the olive oil to drink and do other action like anoint us, we use trumpet, harp, trump and different instrument to glorified God and defeated the enemies that how unique God is how the kingdom operate different from secular world. Normal when the police and solider or security personnel going to fight the enemies they bring guns, tear gas and other protect things to shield themselves. But in the kingdom of God is different we believers use prayer, praise, music and singing of song and silence shut the mouth that what true Christian do. I hear some pastor and member bringing gun for protection and it should not be like that because when Jesus and the other apostle was here on earth, they never have gun protecting them even when some was beaten by the hungry mobs, they never fight back the apostle Paul was beaten partly left for dead and he never fight back. Here come victory song when prophetess Deborah won the enemy the praise God say hear o king give ear we are singing praise to our God for helping us defeat the envies read that worship in judges 5 you can get word from these song and sing them and glorify God there are inspiring song all my reader we need originally song, when you are in the present of God and in praying and have the holy spirit it give you anointed songs, word to preach and dance it in the presence of God the time you spent with him in that prayer closet make you and break you. How I get this book you write I was alone for couple days prayer and fasting and I hear the voice of Jesus say get a pen and paper and start write this book he tells me what to write, in the presence of Jesus lean on him don't let him go like someone you love. Now Gideon and the children of Israel was facing more enemies but again God man get his people to fight, and they blow the trumpet from all side and the enemies was defeated the sound of music read it in judges 7:16 to 18 weapons of worship. I could let this 5 chapter base on the greatest worship of all time king David he write Psalm as you open the bible it psalm most widely read even if you are just starting to read the bible is David psalm so it easy for people to read and see he was a heart worshipper and a true one that he play at fail Saul house and get the evil spirit that was bothering Saul out of him, yes the music of David works that why in truth music draw people together all over the globe I love music big time I listen good music every day.

Ever celebration in the bible is music first when Jesus was born it was praising and worshipper God for the arrival of the *love child* Jesus, the shepherd, the angel and the wise man worship Jesus saying glory to God in the highest peace on earth to all people. We can agree all Christians whether Baptist, seventh day Adventist, Jehovah witness and all the religious group when December come or close to December it the most joyful, happy and most peaceful time of the year that really telling me someone specially was born the king and promise messiah *Jesus* was born. Listen to those Christmas song that play during that time of the year it mind bowling it joy and happiness, last Christmas I was out witnessing here in Florida I met a Jehovah witness young lady she says we don't celebrate Christmas because Jesus was not born on December 25, I told her he may not born on the 25 but he was born, so it not a date we are celebrating we are celebrating a birth. I pray we all get the Jesus spirit that will bring truth to all religious people and let you know Jesus in a relationship style, I remember couple year when Jesus was talking to me, he says be careful of some of these people false religion they are calling my name and I don't know them, I say stop them from falsifying you because some of them are demonic worshipper nothing real about them. God desire true worshipper to worship him in spirit and truth, the sinner women worship look for Jesus and find the Messiah and worship, that Jesus fell this awesome worship and says this women sin is forgiven and she will remember all over the world for her worship what a recommendation from the master himself. I next sinner women from a different country hear about Jesus she not even a jew but she know that sometime in her heart tell her Jesus will help her, her daughter was very sick and the only child she have and desperate for help when she approach Jesus and ask for help first Jesus reply to her I will not give you what I have for the children, but the women reply to Jesus says even if it left over that fall from the table i take it and because of her persistence and steadfast faith and worship her only child was completely heal. Are you desperate for Jesus and his love, peace and joy or you desperate for the thing that can't help you make up your mind what you need? The flesh, the money, the material things will go but the true Jesus is here to stay I hear people say only God salvation last forever., stick with the plan of salvation that is lasting. King David when he just starts getting famous when he come from defeating the enemies the whole Israel come and sing to him say Saul slew is thousand but David slew ten and ten thousand of enemies yes, they keep a praise party for David and king Saul start get jealous of David. Again, be care who is in your circle because when Saul starts to envy David, he was living in Saul house at the time and tell his daughter I am going to kill David because of jealous. But God have a way out for all of us: his daughter tells David you have to leave because my father wants to kill you God give David a way of escape and God is giving you an end route of escape from all who want to hurt you anything he tell you to do go ahead and do it obey.

Jesus is getting ready to shut the door in the devil face tear down is strong hold light him and his demonic agent a fire but continue to worship and praise him in that time of worship everything will be destroy before your eyes. You prayer coming forth your praise coming forth after David destroy the enemies including Saul that want to kill hear his song in 2 Samuel 22:2 *the lord his our rock and my fortress and deliverer in him will I trust he is our shield and the horn of our salvation our high tower and truly our refuge our savior that save us from violence we will all call on Jesus so we know we are safe from the enemies* this song from David will give you the weapon of faith and not worry be brave and passionate. The last word from David just like the last word from Jesus *it finishes man redemption his pay* hear more of David song *the spirit of the lord speak in me and his word was in my tongue the God of Israel said, the rock of Israel speaks to me he that ruled over all people ruling in the fear of God and he is the light that light the whole earth read 2 Samuel 23 get this song in your heart and make melody with these lyrics. Worship transfer when his son Solomon take over the worship continue when Solomon wisdom and knowledge was good because he asks God for it and instantly, he become famous even the queen come and celebrate with Solomon and they keep a feast with all kind of instrument music in all his glory. I see in the spirit people coming all over the world to celebrate Jesus with dance, poem, art work, praise and song of trumpet it going to be millions of people coming in one place like Yankee stadium that how the devil territory will be torn down because of the unity that go into the worship and we going to be one accord get ready for this victory like David. Worship is not mere experience it supposed to be the experience that cannot be erase when the spirit prompts those worship walking, talking, working and the worship in your heart, so when you go to the house of God it pours in with the group worship. Just like you have an exam coming up you study all night and day to pass that exam your brain is sharp to pass, well is the same with God don't wait until you come in the house of the lord to worship do it every day let it be a life style it must be a part of who we are in Christ. When you have true love for each other everything become easy you don't have to force to kiss her because its true love from God, it easy when you really and truly love Jesus you know your duty and happy to give him the best of you.

King David armourbearer marshal of Asaph tell us open your heart to receive the word, the song and the establishment of testimony in the time appointed that the generation to come will know and teach them, they will set there hope in God he is our solid rock a firm foundation we stand he feed us according to the integrity of his heart and guide us by the skillfulness of his hand. So, all my reader doesn't serve or worship any strange God worship the true God of life and light, he arises and judge the earth all the singer and player on instrument shall be there, come all the people let worship and surrender to our God we are his people of his pasture and the sheep of his hand listen and hear his voice and do. Worship the lord in the beauty of holiness, the king Solomon *the door shall be shut no demon and devil shall not come in he is evicted when the sound of music his in gear or you are in fellowship with God no distraction. * We have to teach the people under the manifestation of the holy spirit the knowledge we gave good heed and sought out many proverbs by these all my reader be refresh and admonish because many more inspiring books coming and the spoken word. I like how Paul was admonish his spiritual son Philemon when Paul was in prison he call Philemon his beloved son, God call Jesus is beloved son something about the word *beloved* it arouse you self-esteem knowing we are so much love, so apostle Paul continue to speak to his belove sons *hearing of your love and faith which thou has toward the lord Jesus to all of you that the communication of our faith will be effectual by the regeneration and knowledge of every good things which in Christ Jesus we have great joy in the consolation of his love all God beloved. Read the Philemon all of it very interested.

It does not matter your location these praise and worship and serving Jesus must be lock up in your heart, our body is the church we house the kingdom of God in our body not the physical structure but the spiritual structure. Every time I access God in prayer, I say Jesus I want to be one of main one to house your holiness and I mean it, if you don't mean it don't ask for it just like you start having a family it looks simple on the outside but indeed its great responsibility and commitment, be certain you really and true ready for a family or start a business or get a responsibility job. There are certain things in life you cannot copy like married, people heart and people behavior etc. Be what Jesus create you to be originally even if you are different and unique that okay you would shock how much people want to be like you just because you are originally. I go to the house of God and preacher want to be like me Claudia Henderson they even go further preaching some of the message I preach and get up and leave that what been different is. Some people want the same man I taught, the same cloth I wear, the same friends I taught to, the same gym I go yes, they do, what is for me it will not work for you okay. When you pray and worship and ask God, he will give you what good for you no need to copy people life. Position yourself for your breakthrough it coming pastor rod parsley is good on preaching about breakthrough, pastor mike Murdock is good and preaching about wisdom, knowledge and understanding, pastor td. Jakes is good on preaching get ready, get ready, pastor credo dollar good on preaching about prosperity, pastor joseph prince good on preaching grace and the list go on unique gifting and preaching nothing of this preaching sound alike because they are original foot prints. Tasha cobb good on singing fill me up, Kim walker smith good on singing love have a name, CeCe Wigans good on singing I love you lord, Hezekiah walker good on singing every praise, grace thriller from Jamaica good on singing thank you lord for watching over us and sister Scully good on sing the blood of Jesus, different melody of unique songs original word and songs God gave them, so stop copy people work God will give your own Praise ye the lord praise God in his sanctuary praise him in the firmament of his power, praise him for his mighty acts, praise him according to his excellent greatness, praise him with the sound of the trumpet, praise him with psaltery and harp., praise him with timbrel and dance, praise him with stringed instruments and organs, praise him upon the loud cymbals, praise upon the high-sounding cymbals let everything that hath breath praise the lord. Let praise come from the recessive of you heart and belly. I hear Michael Jackson say in an interview let the music get a whole of you don't go in the way of music and block the flow and after effect of music when it falls hold on to it, be the rhythm of the flow that how the word come to you because of rhythm that fall the die hearted singer will know what I am talking about and producers of entailment. That what in the entailment business you have copy right to protect the original singer of their music, so many time singer and produce sue other singer because they use word from song that not there, I am telling you if music or entailment that what you like you will get your original word and song. I preach because that what I was born to do the word flow in my heart from the spirit and Jesus and it come with uniqueness and different way I do like teach sometime, preach sometime, lecture sometime and prophesy and just be humorous. I know a preacher name bob coy and jess Duplantis these two preachers very humorous preacher, they let you laugh a lot like you go these comedy show. The body of Christ have everything for you to enjoy we don't want you to go back in sin, Jesus need your service, you can record your gospel song we have Christian producers, we have Christian fashion show and gospel concert and movie, we have publisher that can publish your book, we have our own Christian radio and television like: trinity broadcasting network, daystar, word channel, love FM in Jamaica, we have Christian program on Facebook, YouTube, instream, twitter, big o live and all social media platform a lot for believer to enjoy go on make use of them, this writer me Claudia Henderson preach live on Facebook every Sunday at 3pm USA time check us out and I am YouTube have my own channel name Claudia Henderson for more information call: 754 368 9454 we need you to connect with God work. Stop talking Christian life is boring it not boring at all pray about where it happens like where to worship, where these events are, just like you looking for a restaurant, a hospital etc. You would go search goggle, yelp or yellow page apply the same rule with God kingdom the only thing with Jesus is prayer replace these search engines, if when you pray, Jesus says go to these search engines do it but pray before you do this search because it a God business it not like a work place. I am listed on yelp because my motivate is to promote God work, my reason on live Facebook because it was God idea, he spoke to me clearly go there and preach my word I am getting ready for radio and television soon in 202.

I remember when I start to know Jesus' intimate in Jamaica over 26 years one of things, he shows me and tell above radio and television we as believers will be having our own radio and television station and you will be on them preaching. We are chosen man and women special kind we are in the world but don't do things of the world. When David and the people of Israel bring the ark of the covenant the lord tell David only chosen man and women must come and worship before it and give thank that how special we are. Just like you not going to let any and anyone come in your home or circle that how God put a price on us is chosen. So, the worship gets higher when David continues to separate the captain of the host to prophesy with instruction harps, psalteries and with cymbals they were instructed how to worship so you see worship is technical and central. Now all the people bless the lord God of your father bow down and worship the lord anywhere you are shout the praise of God all enemies will be defeated. When God raise jehu, he put his spirit in him and say go and pray and worship and defeat wicked jezebel, she was the one that kill the man for his vineyard we talking about worship that defeated the enemies, which enemies you need to be defeated is it poverty, flesh, sin, drug etc. You can when you pray, worship and pray most important believe your faith fill word will indeed defeat all enemies include dead. Right now, writing this book there is snow storm brewing right here in America but we are praising God it don't happen okay but we are applying the same rule king Jehoshaphat do he pray and the lord tell how to defeat the enemies first he appoint singer not preacher but singer, do you see the important of worship and they worship and go before the army and say thank you lord for your mercy endures forever but the rubber hit the road when they continue to sing God slew the enemies. Read 2 chronicle 19 all to see the how God fight his war. The weapon of our warfare is not cornel but mighty to the pulling down of strong hold, all my reader keep pull it down with your prayer and praise shout out the praise with all you got I watching the television in the gym name planet fitness I see some young lady fighting in the ring but only one win that competition out of 8 of them, so we are winner Jesus is getting ready to crown you and give you, his medal.

So, when the king cup bearer Nehemiah and the children of Israel finish the wall look at the word finish, Jesus say its finish, king Solomon build the temple and it was finish, God create the world and it was finish, make sure you finish what Jesus tell you to do. They keep a dedication service they play instruments and tell God thanks the priest also purified themselves before they go in the finish temple. I am taking you true the different aspect of worship just like you play music at the banquet, at wedding, at the birthday party, at the beach that how we do it in the kingdom of God but our music is gospel and music that have clean lyrics just listen to the word of these song before you play them. All my reader keeps in the arm of Jesus live in him and he live in you meaning have a healthy relation going love on him with prayer or just simple talk to him like you talking to your friends and family and read the holy bible lean on him God created us in his own image. "My foot note: this is my first book so I am not giving you a lot of information but I sure will have more book for you to read in the future more blessing. Amen.

CHAPTER 3:

PRAYER AND PRAISE

"And when he had taken the four beast and 4 and 20 elders fell down before the lamb of God, having every one of them harps and golden vials full of the sweet odor Guess what was sweet odor was Prayer of the Saint."
- Revelation 5:8 to 9

Are sold out Christian praying the Holy Spirit prayer to Jesus so we can get answer, or we are praying selfish prayer with unretentive heart answer this question. We saint of Jesus communicate to Jesus with the Holy Spirit true speaking what the spirit tells us to say God Spirit talking to our spirit and let be obedient and pray so our prayer is answer. The foundation of every believer it does matter our religion is relationship with Jesus we must pray, worship, read God word every day that how we truly grow in Jesus when we connecting in Holy Spirit, Prayer don't have label its word from our heart corresponding to the throne room of grace. Revelation 5:9 that Apostle John writes because he was in the spirit, he could get this revelation of last day the saint prayer pray the right way with Unity and sincerity and ready accepted immediately and after come their worship in sung and praise saying "thou art worthy to take the book and open the seal thereof, thou were slayed and has redeemed us to God by the blood of Jesus of every kindred and tongue, people and nations. Prayer and worship put the devil and his demon flying back to the pit of hell. We have to understand the heart of what Jesus need what we feel like to do in our strength God love is worship big time we can't compromise Jesus' worship for nothing in this world simply give his worship you can be walking, in the shower, driving, at home, at work and worshipping it a matter of the heart that where Jesus judges us from not the outside appearance or the building our heart of to align with Jesus' way of doing things in the kingdom of God. God employ angels 24 hour a day 7 day a week to worship him that how important prayer and worship is. The fall of devil satanic is because he covets God worship and start war against the living God who create him and of course Jesus and his angels lead by Michael and Gabriel and the other waiting angels and they throw in down here on earth in and some of his angels the bible say he come with wrath in his mouth, so don't let the devil deceive you fill your heart every day with the spirit of God so he can't come near us. Anything the devil don't like use it against him holiest, humble, prayer and worship when do it Jesus' way miracle victory every day keep practicing it start now.

Apostle Moses was the greatest prayer warrior in the bible and meekness and humble man ever walk this earth and greatest liberator of human kind every step Moses would pray for what God would need him to do Moses get 1 victory by getting the children of Israel out of bondage hard fight but he won, Exodus 12:51 the same day they were free the people fell in worship and celebration Exodus 15: 1 Then sang Moses and the children of Israel this song unto God we will sing unto the lord for he hath triumphed glorious the horse and the rider he thrown into the sea. When God was going to meet with Moses and the Israelites here come the sound of worship trumpet sounded every step of the way, when Moses was go to God to get the Commandment he fast and pray 40 days and night, when the Israelite sin against it was Moses praying on their behalf for mercy just like write now we are praying that all virus and wickedness come to end in 2020 is same way the advocate ambassador Moses pray, when Moses was chose is elders and minister he pray that Jesus tell who to choose. When Jesus speaks to your personal write it down Revelation 1:19 Jesus speaks to John saying: write the things which thou have seen and the things which are and the things which be hereafter. Make sure we are praying and doing God word because if we are not living Holy here what God say "therefore pray not thou for this people neither lift up their cry nor pray for them neither make intercession for them because I God will not hear them Jeremiah 7:16.

Any place you choose to pray make it be quiet so you can hear obey and do no noise or destruction around I was reading Ronald Floyd on prayer and he say a lady in is congregation every morning 4am she would meet Jesus at quiet spot and pray there, place of prayer can be your bedroom, bathroom, in your car at work anywhere you feel safe and comfortable. Leviticus 16 v 2 and the Lord speak unto Moses and Aaron that they come not at all time into the holy place within the veil before the mercy seat which is upon the ark, that they die not for I God will appear in the Cloud upon the mercy seat, when last you get visit from Jesus just like Moses and Aaron from Jesus or the angels if you are living for Jesus the right way you should get a visit. Some time when I am Fasting and praying most, I don't want physical food to eat because Jesus the Holy spirit fill all you need is to hear his voice and his word let go of flesh and let Jesus Spirit fill your whole body, mind and soul. They're come victory of holiness, unconditionally love, peace that money cannot buy and then husband, wife, money, good health because of your commitment and faithfulness to God. One of my Spiritual fathers in Jamaica say couple year ago Pastor V.T. William when you are anointing of God thing run you down you don't have to run down nothing Jesus will give you when in faith and keep believing. Leviticus 26:7 Jesus shall chase our enemies they shall fall by the sword and 5 shall chase a hundred and one hundred shall put 10 thousand to flight, meaning your loss children coming home, your family coming back home, Jesus is right now cancelling our debt, restoration and healing in your personal life receive what rightfully your right now says thank you Jesus. A Holy Spirit fill life of intensive prayer and fasting bring more blessing in our life and great benefit everything you need from Jesus believe that you receive it. Number 6:22 to 27 let be an addictive praised on purpose not because it out of obligation or is a duty may sure you love Jesus and you do it willfully God know the heart of all of us and our intention and our motivate, the wall of Jericho was an hinderance to God children he instructs Joshua get worshipper and musician and blow the trumpet 7 time for victory some of us would say what trumpet have to do with wall going down it did turn down.

So, anything that blocking your blessing start worship, start praying, start having faith and believe it going right now don't worry or stress out yourself keep open up your mouth and start worshipping the living Jesus now. As believer we have to be in unity on one accord just like the day of Pentecost when the 11 apostle was in unity and receive the Holy spirit same time and they preach all over the world, healing the sick, soul save and restore because of the power of the Holy Spirit.

God use different object to defeat the enemies Moses and Aaron us a simple Rod, Apostle Joshua uses a spear and trumpet, King David uses a stone to take down giants and gangs, Jesus' use candle, olive oil, silva, water simple every day thing we take for granted to defeat this evil devil, Things like prayer cloth, plumbline. So is where these items come from its what Jesus put in it like pool of Bethesda where people go to get healing the angels would come and trouble the water in the pool so it was miraculously just believing all things are possible when we believe and obey order and do. There was a in the bible name Naaman but he was a leper but when he hears of the prophet of God, he and his arm bearer go to receive his healing when Naaman arrive the man tell his maid tell Naaman there is river nearby go wash in that river it was the dirties river in Israel Naaman never want to go in there but is arm bearer tell you need to get well go and he obey and prophet tell dip 7 day and last time he was completely healed. So, anything Jesus tell you to do obey. Obedient is better than sacrifice.

I remember when Jesus tells me 25 years ago go and preach on the bus and train and the high way I quickly obey until present I never tell him that too low because people are everywhere, bus, train, on the road, in work place, in the prison and home go anywhere he send you and don't complain. Some believer telling Jesus where they want to go instead ask him where you need me to go Apostle David every battle he faces with family and enemies he asks God should I go he never do nothing outside the will of God that why he was man after God own heart., humble people are great people. Gideon was a poor Israelite taken from bondage house never in is wildest imagination Jesus would choose him to lead Israelite in the physical no qualification but you see people God was looking at that his heart his style it's what God work with. Gideon turn out to be one of the greatest leader Israel have won all the enemies that come against God children. Jesus chooses people from all position, all background looks at Jesus team of disciple some were peter fisher man, tax collector, Luke doctor, David the Shepherd boy, Rahab the Harlot rich and poor in every one there is good and bad so you are in the will of God whether black, white, rich are poor you are special to God.

2020 and beyond is challenging year for people all over the world but out of a bad situation greatest can be achieve if we only believe, stay positive, optimistic and very important stay focus and alert. Deuteronomy 2:7 Lord thy God have already blessed us in all spiritual blessing by working of thy hand, so the blessing was pay for by sacrifice so access it by faith believing the Lord never leave us or forsake us even why we going true the wilderness meaning sickness, betrayal, abuse, rejection he is still with us. Couple year ago, I watch an interview when Oprah interviewing Whitney Houston she says I sing from my heart not following or copying other even Whitney manager say when first hear Whitney sing, I know she will be one of the greatest singers ever live let me tell until 2020 she is still one of the greatest singers ever live for generation to come unpresented, because it was a gift from God original blue print. Deuteronomy 4:19 and least thou lift up thine eyes unto heaven when see the sun and the moon and the star even the host of heaven should be driven to Worship them and serve them, which the Lord thy God hath divided unto all nation under the whole heaven. Our heart worship is vital important to God not lip service he employs angels to worship him 24 hour a day 7 day a week bear those things in mind and do every day. Faith fill prayer must also be from the heart and having the Holy Spirit with Jesus as result thing will happen as a result of good prayer. Apostle Moses was the greatest prayer warrior 40 days and night without anything eating or drinking committed caring Moses as result of Moses prayer he writes the precept and covenant and commandment to give to the children of God effective prayer answer.

Jesus the high priest of God and son of God pray 40 days and night before he starts his victorious ministry the leader yes Jesus Matthew 4:1 then Jesus led up in the Spirit into the wilderness to be tempted of the devil Jesus fasted 40 days and night but because he prays and fast, he won the devil that the power of Holy Spirit prayer flesh go and the Spirit take over. After Jesus finish pray, he starts picking up his chosen disciples and then Jesus went about galilee teaching in their synagogues and preaching the gospel of his father kingdom and healing all form of sickness and disease among the people. After that prayer and consecration and teaching and miracle he start getting famous not because he Was the son of God but because of the manifestation of the Holy Spirit and miracles that was done. The people follow him everywhere he goes soul start accepted Jesus as the promise Messiah are you seeing these things happen in your ministry if not check your heart to see if you are doing it God way or your way read all of Matthew 4, this ministry is not our way his God way so be obedient to what the master want you to do. Jesus again instructs us when we pray enter into thy closet and when thou shut the door pray to, they father in heaven our father will reward us our motive in prayer of to be unto God he is heart searcher wrong prayer to pray to his unrepentance, wrong motive, praying to hurt people, selfish prayer just you and family those prayer will never answer Matthew 6:5 to 13

Prayer is language every believer should pray the right way every Day pray about everything even who you choose for friends, who you marry, what kind of job you need, where to worship, where to live, what business I should go in, where should I go to school, where should I drive today not all the time the same way or where to walk this morning. There were some many women in the bible Abraham wife Sarah was barren could not have children, Jacob wife Reb could have children, Queen Elizabeth could have children so many women right now cannot have children even present. This special women name Hannah was married but could not have children her neighbor and all who know her would provoke her everyday just like you getting in age and you not married or have children your family or friend would say why you not having a family at your age of course deep down you feel embarrass is same with Hannah, but she take her tear and turn it to prayer day and night no food or water like Jesus and Moses notice all of God chosen man of God they always praying and fasting for anointed and miracle ministry. When false prophets fast and pray the prayer return back to them like this Jezebel fast to kill the man for is vineyard she was envious of his vineyard she and her husband and she get some of the people to pray with her guess what the prayer return back to her and she finally die disgraceful in Israel., check yourself are you praying the right kind of prayer like Hannah Jesus answer prayer and she finally conceive and have Prophet Samuel turn out to be one of the greatest prophet the world I ever seen Hannah get double for her trouble. Now The next Apostle Solomon David son when King David die Solomon was young because he takes over from David but Solomon never knows how to rule people of Israel the principle, he pray to the living God when Jesus appear to Solomon and him what can help with Solomon, he says I am asking for wisdom, knowledge and understanding and God gave Solomon the wisdom and more thing that Solomon never ask for wealth of money the rich ever life and the wisest. Be careful what you ask and petition Jesus for if Solomon did ask for money and wealth in the first place probably, he would never get some much wealth. Yes, you can pray and ask Jesus for money to anything you need he see your motive why you ask for these things and know what you want to do with them that why sometime he simple don't give it to you.

When you look right now in this modern world of all the wealthy people look what some of them do with their wealth and stock, bill latten was wealthy man but he uses his money to kill people, King Saul in the bible was a wealthy man but he never uses his wealthy wisely, so that why some time Jesus can trust with his money, responsibly because you are irresponsible can't handle it. Apostle David moves true the rank before been King when God call him, he still a shepherd boy but not until he won giant, he won gang, he won his enemies including Saul then here God promote David to take charge of half of Israel and then when Jesus test his faith and character more then finally was promoted to the greatest king of Israel. Sometime God just look on an individual and just bless immediately with responsibility, wealth in just split second with let us go true any process because Jesus is just unprogrammed God he knows what to do he created the whole world nobody tell him or dictate to God what to do. Everyone be open mind be alert, stay expecting every day you wake up, This worth mentioning again because the best victorious story I ever hear in a century this poor man in Africa was just hunting in the jungle of Africa when God allow him to find a Jem stone now Jem stone is what make diamond gold and silver the government gave his 7.0 billion dollar from nowhere to somewhere the point he never have work, he never off to study for 20 year he never of go true the process of worker, supervisor or boss God never put true that process he is instant billionaire and then a next young man right here in the U,S.A. use $2 and win $15 million dollar these victorious testimony happen in this 2020. So, everyone keep you dream alive don't let nobody stop what Jesus have for you keep praying and worship God and keep reading the bible set out in faith your prayers will answer if don't give up hope,

This young man right here in the U.S.A was homeless but he keeps praying and he got a add job wasn't paying good but he starts going back to school and keep believing Jesus right now present 2020 at 23-year-old he owns his own business and growing prayer move this hand of God rich or poor not crying or set pitied. This 16 year young lady name Tyla Simone Crayton mother has party but the sauce finish she came up with her own invention putting what she could find in the kitchen of her home and 16 Crayton finally make her own sauce for her mother party right now she make more sauce and sell it to store right here in America and sell one of the biggest store here name Walmart getting ready to go international because she pray and Jesus answer her revenue for 2019 was over $192,000 and growing a little 16 what or you doing with your talent God gave or you sitting on it or you using it to empower other people life. I would encourage you to use it like 16-year-old Crayton. Tennis star serena and Venus William is a perfect example of talent use we all know they were from a poor back ground was rejected by some of the head of Tennis management but there father and mother never take know for answer they train there 2 daughter to be winner in tennis right now is greatest player the world ever see until present Serena and Venus William, our own Usain bolt was the same champion never give up hope from the island of Jamaica dominate the world with his gift of running is the fastest man alive until present, peter Phillip take is gift of swimming to the world and is the greatest swimming the world have ever see, Simone is a next gift of greatest use her talent is greatest gymnastic ever live, tiger wood is next gift of love in golfing just recent won a tournament greatest of all time. I see some much people clean house. Cut lawn for a living and right now they excel to the top because his how we utilize what Jesus put in our heart to do, do and don't say it to simple it doesn't make sense obey our task will finally become our treasure of love and in that process, we bless and encourage other people. Michael Jackson, Whitney Houston and Elvis Presley is some of greatest gift we ever see they share it with us and make us happy sometime I hear people say from these singers die the music industry is shatter is so true we need people to start make it in their heart to use the gift Jesus gave them so other people around them will be happy. We must be happy people full of zeal, passion and happy.

Some people are advocate of the Devil extension there present, the way they talk, they always warring scare you don't it, I personally when I see certain people some time I run or hide because they are devil advocate I sorry to say but is true of course I preach God word to them but when you trying to be friendly, they are nasty so I try not mess too much with them but there are still God children whether good or bad. When I was writing a see a news that I show the epitome of Jesus mercy the women right in the USA Alabama with draw name because of security reason the women was caught stealing food in the supermarket they call the police to arrest her but instead of the police arrest her the police say to her do you have food in your house she say now, the police bring her back in the supermarket buy her grocery and bring her home that how Jesus operate sometime we are guilty but Jesus put you true the women in the bible need justification for her situation in court but she never give up she worn out the judge until one day the judge vindicate her. Persistent don't give up when you personally know Jesus need you to have it go get it to, time to fight for what is rightfully your family, your ministry, your business the is prayer, praise, faith reading God word you need a job, a husband or wife or ministry go get it start go fill out application. Start looking for property to house your church, start going to some decent party, beach social function you can finally meet the man or women of your dread but refuse to sit and relax it don't work like that faith with work is dead, faith and work is recipe to God giving us what we need. Apostle and Prophets was profitable in the kingdom of God give you some: Abel offer more acceptable she receive God children, gift to God than his brother, by faith Enoch was translate and never see death go back to God alive because all these apostle was in the Spirit of God, by faith Noah was warn of God things to come and go ahead and build a ark, by faith this is knock punch Sarah have baby at 90m m yes friend 90 year old, by faith Moses leave the palace of richness and be with his people, by faith Rahab the Harlot was save be she receive God prophets have your faith active you believing Jesus for building for your ministry, you believing Jesus for business, husband or wife don't give up go and social so you see people Hebrews 11 read it about faith and of course you faith will uplift. So next thing stays around positive people even if they are not Christian but they are positive stay around them finally they will come to the Lord because of your influence and impact on their life, opposite avoid negative because they will bring you down to nothing and you will live to regret it, I am making a choice in my life to be with positive people including my ex-friends and right now I glade I did. We need more Holy Spirit mentor, mother, father in the globally body of Christ in the bible the apostle Paul say we have a lot of instructor but not father and mother is a shame are you available for be who Jesus created you to be or you living a life lies answer your question out there, this not even to time of playing around God Business but be true, real, obedient let Jesus be proud of you most time when I see Jesus he always say daughter that tell me a part of the heavenly family and earthy family don't be an outcast be in the house of God and stay in don't lose your place else you will be sorry like disobedient King Saul when he find his mistake it too late Saul even go the seers meaning the witches to help him because Jesus stop talking to him because of his disobedient never take long for Saul to die fighting the enemies but those philistines over throw him, don't end up like King Saul from king to exit from the throne.

Now apostle David take over from the rejected Saul because God was looking for someone humble, faithfully so he send Prophets Samuel for David the next king was chosen 1 Samuel 16:13 Samuel took the oil and anoint him in the midst of his brethren and guess what the spirit that rejected Saul have left him and went into David wow., every

Christian must have the Holy Spirit to be functional and effective it so sad we lose out on Jesus be we never take instruction from God we take from people, that one of the main problems of failure and bad judgment peer pressure of other cause down fall. So, Saul felt the spirit of God left him and he was but to normal he was empty so the evil plaque him he has to send to David to pray for him because you know when you don't have the spirit you like dead man that cannot breathe the spirit of God breathe life let you do extraordinary thing you could do in the flesh. So, man back in Israel try to buy that power of the Holy Spirit form Apostle Paul but Paul tells him this power is not for sale only Jesus cannot give it to you, when you keep holy, stay in the present of God and tarry you will get it eventually make sure you go to temple where they believe in the father, son and holy spirit, as result you must see healing, deliverance, soul save that unwellness of the Holy Spirit. When Jesus was going to his father he tell what the true church and these sign shall follow them that believe in Jesus name you shall cast out devil, we shall speak with new tongue, we shall take up serpent and if we drink any deadly thing it shall not hurt us, we shall lay hands on the sick they will recover, Read it Mark 16:17 to 20 so now when go to the house of God if you don't see these happening that not of go to the pastor show this scripture if he don't do or start doing you can leave and pray to Jesus to lead you where is name is many or call but few are chosen many false prophets gone in the world preaching lie so you are warn in this 20th century read the bible for yourself and let the Holy Spirit teach but still go the bible school but make sure they teach you about the Holy Spirit because indeed that the job of the Holy Spirit comforter, teacher, power source, knowledge source. There was pastor in televise was at the temple but he knows the Special Holy Spirit say go home you and the staff and he close the door and every one leave as they left about couple hour it was big eruption as earthquake the Holy Spirit tell you thing before it happens just like us prophet and apostle and Christian when you connected to Jesus, he tells you the secrets of God. In 2017 there about I was in New York when sweet Jesus appear to me in a dream showing the whole world falling like a tornado he put me on peat stone like a hill and slow me what would have happen in 2018, 2019 now 2020 right now you mass shooting all over the world, plane crash, family missing and right as write this book in 2020 big one corona virus taking the life of some much people all over the world, when preacher predict it must happen there is prophet in the united states name Prophet Caren prophesy 2 year there going be NFL player going to die and COBE BRYAN and his daughter die a right here in Florida show the prophecy he gave on YouTube and radio and television that a true prophets., you see the sign of true prophets it must come to past.

Why Apostle David was super successful after take over from King Saul not because God Choose David but simple because David was faceless, humble, obedient that the qualification Jesus choice I hope you have this character like Jesus, God, David rebellion, flesh disobedient will not let you pass this test but like King David humble The greatest worship and prayer was brother David committed man God and operate in the super natural realm of God he was confident, willing to defend the Great God that raise him up when David see the giant his faith growth big Saul offer David is armor meaning some people expect you must talk like them, pray like them, dress like them but it does not like that with God be original let Jesus tell what to do not pastor or people, so David try it on and it could not fit period so David take order from who appoint God how should I fight this giant and the answer just five stone will do the work no gun, no missile, no knife that will win this specific fight and David do what God say and the 5 stone defeat the giant of Israel., we are defeating poverty, we are defeating flesh, we are defeating racism, we are defeating virus because we do it Jesus way not man way that what giant mean or enemies, starting examining your prayer life your spiritual life, your heart I am at right standing with Jesus let Jesus tell if you are doing his way are your way. Couple month when I finish pray Jesus show some fault of mine so when he shows me right away, I go down on my knee in totally repentance and surrender to Jesus and ask to forgive me Claudia in humble way and thankful way/.

Prayer is way of seeing yourself like a mirror the reflection of who you are and what our way forward not back word so makes sure you pray and worship Jesus every day it worth mentioning. The devil is backward because he don't have a future he get all the opportunities but could hang on to it because of rebellion and envy he was thrown out forceful by the rarifying angel Michael and his awesome team, so don't let him stop your future with Jesus, be alert, vigilant and keep your focus last year 2019 I was in Houston Texas right here United States of America I was really losing my focus and start pray to the living God everyday he is restoring my focus that dangerous when the devil play with our focus and your memory and the big one your mind and soul else you are done big time., safe these sensitive part of your body apply the blood of Jesus on the parts. Our future is Jesus God that our prize position work to please Jesus do everything it take to be in him and Jesus in us, why the say leaves your job Claudia I do because I want to please my master and savior I did when I let go everything was not good but much prayer resilient, reading the word of God not letting my situation dictate to me but knowing Jesus was testing if I love him yes, he knows for sure I love him Jesus. Yes I never past all test Jesus set for me but his mercy enthrone us nobody perfect but Jesus but every day I want to be like Jesus he my greatest idol Jesus when I see how he taught, heal the sick, compassionate even to the thief, the people society rejected he pick us up and clean us off and use for his glory, when he was going true his own trial was humble, gentle, even unto dead the solider at the Cross that inflicted Jesus say when he look in his eyes say truly he was the son of God because he was loving peaceful to dead, we need to pattern this Messiah Jesus and do what he do Love unlimited, forgiveness unlimited. Mercy unlimited read about the greatest man every walk this earth Jesus walk on the water never drown, raise people from the dead, accept us inspire of who we are and where we coming from. Prophet Isaiah, say I say the Lord high and lifted up and trail fill the temple Solomon say the sweet rose of Sharon living of the valley and the light of the world have Jesus in your heart mind and soul and your personal life well never be the same. I as the end time apostle of m Jesus challenge in this 2020 century give Jesus your heart and soul before his too late to put off but do it, my 2 neighbor die one die in height of the pandemic in April of 2020 when the virus just start thank Jesus I share Jesus with both of them so if you are believer reading this book share Jesus with your family, friends, neighbor, coworker do be accountable for not sharing God word Jesus will hold you accountable, don't stand in the ways of sinner be the light they are waiting for whether member, pastor, bishop, elder, minister it does not matter the title you hold in the Kingdom of God open your mouth and share Jesus word., even if you just got save turn around and tell someone Jesus save he keep and satisfy your reward is with Jesus and blessing and sharing Jesus word from I got save and now I am now preaching all over the world start sharing the life word the peace word and the love world.

The next Queen of prayer was Queen Esther was taken in Babylon she lost her mother and father only family member was her uncle Mordecai, The king of Ethiopia wife left him for unknown reason so the king tell his assistant looking around for a next queen, so they gather all the lady all over including queen Esther and the king like Esther and choose her out of all the lady because Jesus favor was upon her try get God favor not man so Queen Esther was jew by origin but she never let the king know the time never right for that secret to reveal. So, before Esther could talk to the king, she has to go true a period of purification meaning repentance, holiness, sanctification how to talk there rule how they do thing in the palace., just like when you just got save it take a time drop bad habit like lying, cheating, gossiping etc. So there was wicked man in the place hate Esther name Haman and want to destroy him and the other Jewish people there it like we have family, coworker that want to destroy us but they can't do it but when Esther hear about the plot she call her uncle and they start a 3 days fasting and prayer notice Esther sees answer back with fire of destruction., I see people come against me big time and I pray to Jesus in sincere way and when I see The result I was shock Jesus he defend his son and daughter everyday don't fight your battle pray like Esther, David, ruth us prayer warrior Jesus will surely vindicate you successfully. Ho hurt Guess Queen Esther end up marrying to the influential King in that region but God say keep believe even in jail, prison in the hole Jesus will come true for you just keep believing like us. Make sure we have an open heart with love, caring, sharing at right standing with Jesus not I contrive heart, not envious heart your prayer will never answer most forgive who hurt you okay you need Jesus talk to you well do what please him Jesus, you never see me so you have to lean to forgive who see every day and live peaceable and share what you have with them don't be selfish. Isaiah 58:5 and 6. Prophet Jeremiah the youngest prophet chosen than all the prophet pray saying Lord for I know the thought that I think say the Lord though of peace and not evil to give us expected end, then shall ye call upon me and ye pray unto you Jeremiah 29:11 to 12 true prosperity God gave with no string attack so demonic people offer you position or money for sex you can't help yourself you give in and after everything said and done you end up with life threating disease and the boss end up fire after you take the position so why not hold on tell Jesus that give you the perfect gift of Godly jobs, family that last forever until least Jesus not take it back from you have for life even God gave you a gift to sing, preach, heal people even if you sin against him he not taking back from you wait on Jesus be patience don't be anxious for nothing and then say you are sorry. When I use work with the Police department in Jamaica my job there was take care of office part of the department what thing I can tell you when they bring in the inmate one thing all of them say "if I did know" when is too late so do let when Jesus come you say the same if I did know I would heed to the preacher and serve God when it's too late.

Me talking about prayer in this chapter and worship which every believer should do that have personal relationship with Jesus not religious, The Next Apostle Daniel was also in exile like Esther when he was chosen to set Israel free the transforming Holy Spirit was in Daniel every chosen apostle have the Holy Spirit and Kind love Daniel because the king see Jesus on Daniel like joseph, David ruth, Esther you transfer of favor and grace take time read this book soon you can see the important of what God will give you. So when the other worker see the king love for Daniel they start fight against Daniel prayer for is enemies and God favor increase in his live they go that far to throw in the lion den to get ridded of Daniel but he was not afraid because he have relationship with Jesus he Daniel was surely save the King say to Daniel I need you God Daniel are you show off Jesus anywhere you are at home, vacationing, on the job some time you don't have to talk people must see Jesus in you all over you it come with calmness, over flowing love, caring and sharing that how people will ser Jesus because o no illumination your action because obviously they don't see Jesus in person so Jesus in you will bring them to the cross get this in your spirit., be Jesus mouthpiece, be his hand and his disciples of promise like Daniel and 3 Hebrews boys never bow. When you have healthy relationship with Jesus when the devil come to tempt you know right away you answer is known don't want it not bowing to the devil level, if Jesus would have taken is throne I don't think anybody would have left on this earth try don't work for the devil work for God he is the one make the devil so why you serve him because you are gluttonies evil eye cant satisfy my mother vie would say you children need to satisfy with what provide in my house it m so true some time you end up in great trouble because you could not wait like so many people lose everything house, cars, family and loose on Jesus.

Worship God even when it does not make sense addiction and good ability is what Jesus need in worship not just when you are in the house of God but worship in our heart 7 day a week 24 hour day is what Jesus desire some time nobody have to hear but you and God private worship, Private prayer sending time with Jesus that how he knows who you really are not pretending to be what you are not at church you can pretend to be holy and righteous but when you are alone it totally different. I use to live with a church sister of mind I was shock at her behavior at the house of God perfect but when she is at home is different, I have to end up move out because of her behavior that why I know for sure and learn from the n word of God how Jesus Judge. Just like back in those day in some of the Israelite that call themselves Pharisee and scribes was great pretender of fake Christian kill prophets like Stephen stone the holy man God to dead and many until present see the news where in country, they light this woman of God to dead with she was Christian some thrown in jail, rejected and abandon. I surely being a lot myself which I mention in the first Chapter betrayal, rejection, homeless, abuse but never give up on Jesus because the connection is we all go true it to Just like Jesus. Stay pray up stay encourage stay in the present of God Jesus love just the same good time and bad time. Just like you marry the original vow say for better or worst real God love is good time and bad time, sickness and good health but in this age of computer they change the wedding vows to suit their condition of thing. That why is very important to pray before you marry or do anything. Last year 2019 when I was in Texas USA when I finish pray and sat there waiting for Jesus to answer me he show me a lot of American flag and say pray for America couple month I finish pray again sitting waiting for Jesus to answer my prayer Jesus come himself and say daughter you are well cover He have umbrella in his hand cover with the umbrella that blesses assurance our savior and lord for us is children the Spirit and relation let you see God glory Jesus was radiant in his priestly grown looking radiant that experience I will treasure every day of my life.

In summer of 2017 I was in New York doing mission so I work early to do my prayer as my normal routine I try to wake early like early morning turn of all noise unless his your worship music I like from 1a,m morning cool nice quiet and romantic, so that specific morning I was worshipping here come Jesus flying over me and talking in eloquent voice saying look down there some money for you he was with me for quite a while it was like somebody give me a Billion dollar that while I try to stay in the Spirit of God to experience Jesus for yourself. I typing this manuscript and just over whelm by his present because in the first it Just idea for me to write this timely book thank you Jesus, couple year I try to write a book when I just arrive in the USA but I end up misplace the manuscript because it was not time to write. This time Jesus says get you pen and paper and start write you best seller book call "our Mess become our Message of Love" Jesus gave me even the title of this book the design and I know you are blessing and encourage be this timely book not any and any book but this real inspiration book from the author of love. Be heir of is inheritance serve Jesus faithfully continually my Pastor in Jamaica always say you are excellent worship I lean in the kingdom of God give Jesus the best not second-best Jesus gave his best for us did he yes, he did all for us. What I notice with all these successfully gospel artist including Grace Thriller a group we growing on in Jamaica, Marian Hall, Tasha Cobb, CeCe Winna, Kirk Franklyn, Kim Walker smith, Judah Jacob, Hezekiah walker, Marvin providence, Sandra brooks, Eddie James just recently hear Eddie James and love this prayer son. Denis brown, bob

Marley, Tremaine Hawkins, Charles Jenkins to name of few most these singer sing about the Holy Spirit that why most of their song are chart buster hit do very good on the international chart, most Holy Spirit Preacher including TD jakes, Benny Hinn, John Hagee, Errol Blair, VT William, Paul Lewis, Joyce Meyer, Belford Davis, Apostle Maldonado, some of simple people that preach on the bus on trial bless too because that how I start preaching on bus or train in Jamaica so I have field of preaching before I start preach on the bus it was my pleasure to listen these bus preaching never knowing Jesus would choose to start my ministry on the same buses and train. Right now, I taking this message all over the world on same bus, train, churches little things lead to greatest I am enjoying this mission God gave not pastor gave but Jesus himself give like Apostle Moses call in the wilderness and Apostle David call at his house so pastor don't have call the best call his Jesus choose you. Next prophet that prays effective was Zephaniah see the judgment of Judah under king Josiah when Zephaniah talk with God, he says for we will famish all the false Gods of the earth and men shall worship him God. Read Zephaniah 2:11 right now in this broken world let pray against oppression, depression, racism, abuse, partially, illicit flesh, against lying, false religion, against poverty, right all over the world Jews and Christian are celebration "Day of Atonement" meaning asking Jesus the sacrifice Lamb that was slain gave is life for sin we as Christian must stop sinning and for those who as not yet give their heart and soul over to Jesus is full time you make a commitment to serve Jesus receive the gift of life. Leviticus 23:26 to 27 And the Lord spoke unto Moses saying, also on the tenth day of the seventh month there shall be a day of Atonement: it shall be an holy convocation unto you, and you shall afflict your souls, and offer an offering made by fire unto to the lord., and ye shall do no work in that same day for it is a day of atonement, to make an atonement for you before the Lord our Great God, Leviticus 23:37 tell the different we give an the altar in this season of atonement feast of the Lord which we shall proclaim to be holy convocation to offer an offering made by fire unto the Lord: a burn offer, meat offering, drink offering, trespass offering and thank you offering. So, if you are relationship Christian you should observe this day every year in September and search yourself if you are pleasing Jesus that most important.

We are blowing the trumpet right now anywhere you are because we are free black or white sometime, we are enslaving in our mind, in our heart and some case in physical prison but when we learn to worship and praise God, we literally be free location does matter Jesus must live in your heart to get true freedom, especially in this season of atonement it real time of celebration of triumphant. The character of Jesus fruit he demonstrates here on earth is unconditional love not sex, peace, joy, caring, giving, Jesus do lot of miracles and he preach the gospel of his father God and many people was save, heal, save on deliver are we seeing these things happening where we worship check to see if it not happening go to pastor ask him, he what happen to the Holy Spirit and miracles. Next prophets pray was Malachi he is call Socrates because he use the style specialist in rhetoric, this prophet pray for financial blessing on God people and ministry and teach of the love God have for his people and ministry Malachi speak to the Israelite saying Israel I love you saith the Lord yet ye say wherein hast thou love us and now I pray you beseech God that he will be gracious unto us, has been by your means will he regard your person saith the Lord of host., Malachi pray and beseech God for backslidden and tell they must give there Tithes and offering will you rob God you rob people and get away but when you rob Jesus you are in big trouble, meaning you don't give tithes and offering we must have to give that how you blessing come hear what Malachi 3 v 8 will a man rob God, yet ye have rob me in tithes and offering you are curse with curse for you never give God is money even the whole nation is curse because don't give God Malachi 3:10 read for yourself Bring ye all the tithes into my storehouse that there be food in my house to feed the Pastor, members, missionaries and pay the bills in the house of God and of course feed the poor and help his preach God word all over the world start give money, give good word, give a compliment give a word of encouragement. When you give Jesus 10% here the blessing he open the windows and pour is blessing on our churches, our family our coworkers everyone round you will be bless because you entertain God blessing by obeying is command, your enemies shall not touch you, all nations shall call you bless no sickness shall take out not even corona virus, start shouting alleluia, praise you Jesus, Thank you lord you take care of me and my family Read all of Malachi and see Jesus financial plan for your life. Next Prayer is of Habakkuk the minor prophet God raise up Habakkuk to pray the enemies that form themselves against God children Jesus defend is chosen people on till today so we don't have to fight physical all we need to fight spiritual in prayer and fasting and worship read God word, the prophet hear God word and was afraid but he ask Jesus to revive is good work, are we out there as believer are praying and fasting for revival to see soul save from doing wrong thing, do we care and really love Jesus that much to go in street, in mountain top, in train and bus, in our work place and family and tell them face up Jesus Save, well if say you love Jesus be is hand and mouth piece work for him that what going to prove that you love not just word Singer <Michael Jackson) say word is cheap. When I say Jesus, I love you with my heart it never takes long for me to start share him with other including my own family until present do the same and stop gossip and lie and do evil., get moving for Jesus be his messenger is pickup driver and deliverer driving.

Jesus have me Claudia Publish this book knowing in this 2020 so many bad things happen we all need to be encourage I can assure you Jesus is rescuing right now don't stress yourself out, don't panic have faith in God and trust the Lord with all your heart and learn not to your own understanding lean on Jesus, if lean on self you will surely fail and be miserable. All of these apostles, preacher, teacher never lean on themselves they whole hearted lean on Jesus God for clear direction do the same and take it one day at time be patient. So when Jesus Blessing come in your life share he give us to be selfish take care of it too else it will fade away., we got to know these fact on Jesus that he was 100% man and 100% God he go true pain like us, rejection, his was crying like us some of his own people reject him and say you is not the promise Messiah even dough they see the miracle he do raise the dead, heal the sick just recently in April or March of this 2020 A retire Police was hit by corona virus right here in the USA but he never stop pray they release from the Hospital to go home when he go he have to come back to hospital he could breathe the cove 19 hit your breathing that why so much people dies from this deadly sickness, the man say when he come back to the hospital about in the wee hours of the morning about 2am He say Jesus come and start pump fresh air in his mouth and after the miracle Jesus say to him you are completely heal ask the doctor to release and yes he go home., are you still believing Jesus for you miracle are you give up I hope you don't give on Jesus. I was personal heal from Ovaries Problem, Back pain, stress and depression on anxiety just believe the master he will do it for you amen, Prayer and praise must be our life like the blood in our body flowing in to different organs that how prayer and praise was circulate in our heart and soul subconscious., I remember couple year I was at work in Jamaica I was there secretary for the company so when the phone ring instead I say hello The worship just flow out of my mouth subconscious was planning on answering the phone with a praise but I was charge that morning from home to work no room for the devil your praise and prayer holiness and humbleness chase him away, because that what run him out of heaven in the first place, listen if someone come by you home and tell the person I don't want you coming at my home it a clear point you make, just like the devil he cannot go back on God throne period he has an unwelcome guess., so continue chase him with your praise. Before I was Christian I love music party, club, wedding anywhere joyful people I would be there especially good loving music so it naturally when Jesus save my soul over 25 year I came in the body of Christ still loving music especially love music Whitney Houston love son, Luther Vandross, Denis brown, bob Marley, Kim Walker smith and of course Michael Jackson you see Christian listen to some of these music you can sing them it all of love not miraculous so don't be judgmental but spent to read the bible and ask the Holy Spirit to teach you and interrupt for you, you can drink a little wine at home not the bar but don't overdo it about the win read john 2:2 to 11 and see these thing is ordain from the beginning stay away from judgmental Christian there is gym I work out in right here in Florida name Planet Fitness there motto is don't be judgmental but be reserve. We need to settle down relax, and say Holy Spirit, Jesus teach me to be like you instead of liking gossip news and like attack character that the devil playground we talking about judgmental there was women in the bible she was caught in the act of adultery meaning she was with a marry man someone wife but when the judgmental people in Israel come to stone her Jesus was on the ground praying to our heavenly father how should I rule this case, hear what Jesus say to people who want to kill the women any one of you don't have a sin cast a stone all of them was a shame throw the stone and left only Jesus and women was still there, hear they the conclusion of this ending store Jesus say with a merciful love go lady and sin no more., so be careful how you judge people pray to Jesus for an answer instead of be hasty.

I can relate to people story because I Claudia be true so much abuse, betrayal, poverty, rejection, they rob so much time even when was writing this book august 2020 I went for walk in my neighborhood was rob of my phone end up in hospital with minor bruise, homeless right here in the United States, But I never let go of Jesus hand sometime very discourage like you do but still pressing on., 2019 I was Houston Texas doing mission they have major hurricane in that state lot people loss everything I went to a church there I hear a lady giving her testimony she and her husband loss everything house car, but her victory testimony was Jesus restore back everything because she believe he would and she was vindicated, this 23 year man right here in the USA was homeless but he never give up hope and right now in 2020 he own his own business at 23., never give up your prayer will answer if it pray the right way. Wrong prayer that don't get answer Isaiah 58:4 behold he fast for war and debate and smite with the fist of wickedness, he shall fast as he do this day to make your voice to be heard on high in v 4 It such a fasting and prayer that I have chosen a day of atonement for us afflict our soul bow your head as bulwark and spread sackcloth and ashes under us, thou will call this day an acceptable day to the Lord., in 6 as we fast an pray against wickedness, undo heavy burden, no more racism, murder, missing people, no more gossiping etc. every from yoke of bondage Next blocking why our prayer cannot answer Isaiah 59 v 2 but you iniquities have separated between you and your God and your sin have hid his face from you Jesus will not answer you prayer your sin include your hand are defile with blood, your finger with iniquity, your lips have spoken lies, your tongue had muttered perverseness, non-call for justice no truth pure lie, they conceive mischief and bring forth iniquity., so check your heart if you are guilty of the sin and surrender to Jesus and ask forgiveness now before you read more. Matthew 17:21 sometime these demonic spirits come out be prayer and fasting some time it takes 1 day prayer and fasting some time again it takes 3 week or more wrath of prayer and fasting to get rid this demon. The church in New York where the famous Brooklyn Tabernacle Choir sing the wife of the pastor say she have to pray for many year before her husband was finally save but she never give up right now they have one of the largest church in the world there anointed choir sing all over the world I was living in Jamaica when they come and sing for the people of Jamaica of course they do great job singing so don't give up even if you got to wait for 20 year it worth waiting but don't compromise else you will end up sorry. When you make sacrifice for Jesus you will never lose out if family gone like job in the bible keep wait, if loss your house car, business family Jesus will repay you 3 time of one your loss like the women in Houston Texas. Matthew 19:29. Holy Spirit prayer from Jesus is knock punch to the devil strong hold pray that prayer every day and stand in faith believing for the result 2019 I was in college park Georgia I was witnessing but I remember I saw a man sit in his car and I approach with telling him about Jesus he say sister I am Pastor but every day the people come they left my reply to the estrange pastor search your heart what you doing wrong and go into some prayer and fasting for Jesus to answer I was sarcastic in my answer but that truth I tell him, couple year I went to Miami to church service my first time in that temple the service was so boring I felt I was at a funeral I travel to a lot of Church and some I will never go back because Jesus is not there is just the flesh and there way of doing that wrong., let Jesus tell you where to go worship so many satanic temple building be careful where you go the church is a place of prayer and hospital not work place or organization. We must see the manifestation of Jesus miraculous power in our life, our ministry and family, this is a fivefold ministry consist of pastor, apostle, prophets, teacher and help which gift you receive from Jesus: operate in this gift effectively., in all we do in body of Christ we must be humble servant Jesus say we must be humble more grace to the humble and be obedient in how we operate than why the devil fall be the start getting prideful and rebellious against God and was thrown out.

Apostle Paul was a recipient of the getting the Holy Spirit and his live was transform instantly from been slanderous to been Jesus chosen vessel Paul end up travel and preach the glorious gospel all over the world and write most of New Testament. Every believer should have the Holy Spirit it was from the beginning that how you will pray, praise God and hear the secret of Jesus because of the Holy Spirit that transform our life into the super natural realm of God. Genesis 1:2 states earth was without void and darkness was upon the face of the deep and the Holy Spirit move upon the earth. Now worship enhance Jesus's glory there was a woman in the bible she was a sinner but she worships Jesus buy her expensive oil and anoint Jesus and most importantly she worships with her whole heart, mind and soul and Jesus say because of her worship she will remember and the gospel is preached because of these generous women and right away her sin was forgiven. Look and the outsider Father Abraham, this unsensed women and ruth was from a different nation that never believe in God like the Jewish nation but Jesus look in there heart and use to accomplish a lot in the kingdom of God it a heart thing not where you come from or the color of our skin some of his Jewish people never worship like these outcast, Jesus m went to his own his own receive him not but strange people receive him it a shame when you own family, your own Christian people don't receive your but most important Jesus accept you in is family of embrace, are we as believers defendant Jesus ministry are we defendant our own answer this question? Look at the pattern when Jesus enter the temple the people was gambling of all place in the house of God but throw out all the gambling money and tablet and declare this is my father house of prayer not casino house with power we must always defend Jesus commandment, Statues and covenant and stop defend position, title in the kingdom Jesus ministry is not a position, professional, title ministry is HOLY SPIRIT ministry from God with no label on, the devil play ground is title, position and profession if you have the Holy Spirit he show all you need to know about how the Kingdom of God operate so try and get the Holy Spirit. After Jesus all out good deed, miracles the whole nation come and honor him saying Hosanna blessed is he who come in the name of the Lord Israel get Jesus a sendoff worship and adoration anywhere you are start worshiping Jesus for the Great King he is in our daily life praise Jesus.

Jesus speaks to us true dream, people that he chose or verbally voice so we must listen and obey what he wants us to do don't caught up with everyday life and be busy all the time but spent time with Jesus we can be like him every day, sometime when Jesus speaking to me and I don't remember I cry Jesus remind me what you were saying that very important to listen and write and do. When I was writing this book in 2019 the news was so bad terrorist kill over 290 people injure over 500 in the country name Sri Lankan including church building, hotels, We see school shooting in New Zealand, plane crash in Indonesia, tornado in Africa, fire in California Presently in 2020 we are battling the deadly corona virus and the up serge in racially war right here in the USA so many people loss there life., so we need to start pray more time per day and worship and share Jesus Holy Word it urgent we do if you are a believer and care. Jesus is right now releasing your chain because me pray fervently live are be save and we are rescue from Satan scheme of evil keep focus on the God that his able do exceedingly abundantly all that we ask and more only believe. There was Paul and Silas was preaching and the evil people put them in jail for preaching God word but they never panic they pray in the jail cell and at mid night Jesus send the angel to free them that prayer in action and was answer immediately if you don't pray to Jesus he can't help us prayer have to pray and ask for what you need, Jesus say ask and it shall be given unto you seek and you will find so open your mouth and start praying for what you need and stop crying and stressing out yourself.

Jesus comfort us in all tribulation it does not matter what we are going true pain, suffering and sickness Jesus loving arm is all over us He comfort us in all tribulation go ahead and pray with other share God word and comfort them when Jesus bless us turn around and bless other don't be selfish that us make the world a better place by giving, share, loving not sex but give God word and be friendly with each other be our brother keeper., check on your neighbor, check your family and coworker the burning candle stick the people need to see not been mean and aggressive and always warring else we don't want to see you around because that Satan character he come to kill, steal and destroy but Jesus come to kill live more abundant so choose Jesus everyone. Jesus is the one that give true promotion not your Boss, nor your Pastor is Jesus read Psalm 75:6 for promotion cometh neither from the east, west nor from the south, but God is the judge he putted down one and settled up another so when they fire or tell not come back in the temple like how they do Jesus and us don't feel bad Jesus has big open door for you in 2020 and beyond sometime that the Jesus move us to high dimension in life, because we don't want go so he allow the boss to fire or preacher tell you to go He getting ready to giving you your own ministry, your own business, your own husband and wife pray to Jesus for clear direction on your future only Jesus speak the truth and originally word. Align yourself with God word and do for year some Christian believe is Jesus only some other religious group just believe in only God but the true is God the father, the son Jesus and the special Holy Spirit The send his Son Jesus to be our advocate for true salvation and sacrifice for us all because the animal blood could not pay for our sin anymore and teach us the way to God that Jesus function, the Holy Spirit is what teach us the deep secret of God and feed us wisdom, knowledge and understanding that the function GOD is the creator that made all thing in heaven and earth the only true creator amen so you learn the operation of the Trinity read it 1 John 5:6 to 12. When you feed on God Holy word every day you will learn and do them daily Apostle Joshua say meditate on God word every day let the word be in our heart so we may not sin against God. We are no more in the darkness anymore the Great light Jesus has come illuminate our soul accept this Great light of Love, resurrection, restoration, Happiness and peace start shout for victory and freedom at once you Blessing is here financial blessing, salvation for you and family, you looking for a building to put your church is your, act in faith and work no longer lack and despair only believe all thing are possible when you believe. When I was a young kid, I dream of travelling the world like all of you people thank Jesus I am travelling all over the world preaching Jesus Holy Spirit word and, in the process, see the world for who it is beautiful we are God children we must live in the best house, drive the best car, have the best family because we are is children.

Jesus our high priest never found with no sin or done anything wrong but he takes on our sin so we can be in right standing with God, what a love demonstrates on earth Jesus take our place so we can be righteous before God and accepted in his family without be rejected because of our sin Jesus take it all of us say out there thank you Jesus for being our mediator between man and God. Jesus Love Glorify, justify, ratify and purify our heard all day read 1 / 2/ 3 near revelation about true love not fake love. Same John say try all the Spirit because some spirit is not of God be careful of the Spirit you have the true spirit confess Jesus that Jesus come in the flesh of God that true Spirit and false Spirit say Jesus never come in the flesh read it in 1 john 4:2 to 3 The truth about Jesus is finally revealing true love is of God no exchange in God love no performance, no merit you don't have to do anything extra ordinary to get God love no money, no fame can buy Jesus agape love black or white, rich or poor, good or bad Jesus love you he bled and die on the cross so we can have great life that why we have so much broken relationship because is money love in the first place, or position love, or fame love meaning you have to have fame, money to get love that demonic love satanic love don't enter the love it dangerous my mother and father marry and live for so many year over 30 year tell my mother die, met lady tell she and her husband live for over 60 year in married and still going strong so when you getting make sure it for love of God in good time and bad time is love money are no money is love get with Jesus love not the world love.

Jesus have 12 Apostle but when Jesus was going to do is Great assignment only 3 he would bring Peter, James and John be they we having the same Spirit, so be careful who is in your circle who are your arm bearer, who you let in your house, who is your friends that most important because is who near to you have access to what you have Judas and Peter betray Jesus when he need them most but Jesus forgive them Judas end up kill himself., we must pray about everything and you will be safe all the time. Apostle Paul Mentor Titus and Timothy in the ministry Paul tell them what should be done and how it should be done Jesus they were people obedient when Paul was in jail its timothy take over church and he connect with in jail and they obey they pray and worship God because of good mentoring. So be careful who mentor you out there wrong mentoring cause war in the body of Christ in one instance King Saul mentor David and then turn around and fight against him be watchful in prayer and praise and meditation. Apostle John sees the amazing worship in heaven the elder, the angels, the beast and worship like there no breathe left that kind worship Jesus desire true worship from the heart not lip service., say glory, honor, power, to the great God. This specific chapter is about prayer and worship so read this book spent time and worship God don't rush it reading this book you believe you can receive your miracle of healing, deliverance and salvation people from all nation stood before God who sit on his throne with Palm in hand waving more worship salvation to our God thanksgiving glory to our God.

Relationship with Jesus very important not crazy religion limitation when religion take you over but when you come to that place of true relationship with Jesus you are in greatest with him John was in the spirit to see everything that would take place in the last day it happens now in 2019 and 2020 if some of still alive you will see more thing happen in the last day. I saw a new on Facebook this baby just born tell his mother JESUS is coming soon I believe The Baptizer John talk when he was just a baby that the greatness of Jesus is all in believe everything in God Kingdom is believe and receive do you out there believe Jesus for what you need from poor to rich, from sick to heal, from dead to life simple you believe. The couple share their resurrection story on face they were in a car accident both the doctor pronounces them dead but Jesus come in that Hospital and blow life in them and come back to life just recently so many resurrections story of God goodness so start believing for your miracle stop doubting God is speaking are we listening or doing or we ignoring Jesus' word.

Keep in Jesus and Jesus in you be proactive be optimistic be committed, be faithfully let your mind stay on Jesus don't let the world consume us away from what Jesus have for you no distraction. The bible says if you are friend of world, you cannot please Jesus we are in the world but not doing what the people of the world do meaning no lie, no cheating but live holy Keep yourself in prayer and praise and reading God world seek the kingdom of God all thing will be added unto you husband, wife, job, miracle money and Holy Spirit ministry Just trust Jesus and get is wisdom, knowledge and understanding.

I need to end the prayer a praise chapter with a praise song and a prayer: "For you I live Jesus to worship you O praise the Lord all ye nations, praise him all ye people, for his merciful kindness is great towards us and the truth of the Lord endure forever, praise ye lord everyone. Psalm 117 I Pray a Prayer for all my fans and readers: Thank you Jesus that you afford us precious life inspire of all that happen all over the world you still love us unconditionally, you still heal everywhere it hurt spiritual, physically, emotionally and physiologically you are so great, good, perfect, loving that Jesus we are your price possession. Heal, save, deliver every one reading this book in Jesus' name we pray in care of The Especially Holy Spirit. Amen.

CHAPTER 4:

THE HOLY SPIRIT EVERY BORN-AGAIN BELIEVER SHOULD HAVE

"The spirit of the lord is upon me because he has anointed use to preach good tidings unto to the meek, he sent us me to bind up the broken hearted to proclaim liberty to the captives and opening of the prison to them that are bound." - Isaiah 61:1

The holy spirit is the channel to known Jesus and his righteousness and God indeed, God is a spirit and they that serve and worship God must have the spirit of truth some places you go we must wear a mask don't it the spirit is a must as believers so go ahead a get the spirit so we can see the thing of God we access Jesus in the spirit not in flesh. Genesis 1:2 the earth was without form and void darkness was upon the face of the deep *the spirit of God move upon the face of the earth*, so we see the prove that the holy spirit create and build the heaven and earth building the foundation of all believers the power of the holy spirit take the wait of us when we solely depend on the spirit not our own intellect it will fail. So preacher would tell I don't worry about what to preach and how to get money to build the house of God because they always access the holy spirit and Jesus to do all you need to do show up at where you want to build, show up at the interview, show up at the house spot where you knew home will be build, show at the party or the wedding, show up at the airport and God will buy your ticket to get on that plane, that you know God is getting ready to give you a husband and wife the big word *show up* a word of knowledge I writing this book under the manifestation of the holy spirit and Jesus just giving me the word to give to you all receive this now word and do it put it in action my brother and sister and stop worry be bold and courageous.

Because the spirit was present to create God the owner created the world perfectly, do you see the important of the spirit even God in all is greatness of to depend on the holy spirit, when he made Adam to maintain the earth, he knows Adam need company so he let Adam go in a deep usually sleep and take the bone from Adam and create the female eve, so he told them maintain and take care of the earth. God gave them specific instruction there are certain tree in that garden don't touch it, when God exit the property, the female eve encourage the man Adam to touch it so when Adam touches its God know something wrong because when God came back in the garden, they were naked and ashamed that first became the fall of human kind because of disobedient and sin. Before they sin, everything God created was super perfect nothing was missing and nothing was lacking but disobedient people until present cause sin here an earth. Why we have some much sickness and disease because they provoke God with idol, ate the sacrifice of the dead, we complain every day, the put themselves together with the enemies like king Saul, they shed innocent blood and they continue to sell their body for money and take the devil money those things cause curse and destruction. From the 20th century to 2022 we see all over the world plane crash, virus, sickness at its highest level, tornadoes, hurricane, the cycle of weather change it turn out to be disastrous, we see senseless shooting, domestic violence at its highest rate. What we are saying sin and disobedient cause this tragedy. We are still talking on the spirit but this prophecy is very important to your knowledge, when God take the children of Israel from bondage in Egypt in care of Moses and Aaron some of the same Israelite rebel and sin against God for nothing God done to them by freeing them. Just like you are peaceful and loving but some people just keeping messing with you for nothing that the same thing with the children of Israel behavior so because they sin God allow some of them to die in the wilderness because of their action of disobedient and complaining and sin. The holy bible says the wages of sin his dead by the gift of God is life choose life and not dead is when you sin you get a dead sentence from God just like in the court of law when you do wrong thing the judge sentence you don't it. The priest Aaron his sons make strange fire at the altar before God they die, king Saul disobey God instruction and the enemies kill him, samson the strongest man in all the bible marries strange women that God disapprove and the pageant women conspire against his husband samson and he end up dead. We need to stop sin meaning for those who don't know what is sin it doing wrong thing like: lie, steal, kill, fornication, adultery, conspiring to hurt, manipulating etc. When we change and stop, and start serving Jesus we see peace, more love, no more disaster in this present world. We have 2 force operating God which he is good and great, and Satan which he is so bad no one should entertain him. You entertain the devil by doing wrong thing and have bad habits, we entertain Jesus by accept is salvation, is love, peace and joy my fan and reader chose who you want to serve and entertain in this 2022 century and beyond knowing we are at the end of this present world. The topic: <u>the holy spirit righteousness</u>: not by work of righteousness which we have done to earn the favor of God, but according to his mercy he saves us by washing of regeneration and renewing of the holy spirit Titus 3:5 him whom we trusted we heard the word of truth the gospel of your salvation in whom also after that ye believe we were seal with that holy spirit of promise we are not seal with the devil 666 but Jesus' seal and cover us with is seal approval Ephesian 1:13. Of which the prophets have inquired and search diligently who prophesied of the grace that should come unto us, keep ourself in the presence of God be on the alert in the spirit be sensitive. Peter 1:10'. The <u>holy spirit that raise up leader and apostle</u>: we start with preacher Noah a man approve by God to warn the evil wicked generation in those days people were sinning bitterly now Noah was preaching salvation to the people even now we are the continuation of preaching God word in this 20th century until Jesus return make sure you are preaching and sharing God word like Noah the man of God preach for year the people mock him and make fun of him, God tell Noah build a ark because I about to move yes Noah build the ark and preach at the same time even thou they see the ark they still keep sinning and do evil the ark was finish. God tell Noah get every pair of animals and your family and go in the ark, animal take the place of sinful man it ashamed people until now chose to do evil, the rain came and all of them was drown in the flood. That what is going to happen now if people don't repent and turn from there evil ways God send his precious son Jesus to reconnect back with God, serve Jesus before he come back., when Jesus come back we better be ready not getting prepare but be ready just like you going on bus or plane make sure you get there before the plane or bus take off, the good thing about God after the apostle complete is assignment God tell him Noah now go be fruitful and multiply and populate the earth so I am saying go do good thing for Jesus like Noah go share, go witness, go pray, go mentor someone that need your service, go volunteer okay, we are the continuation of Noah, Jesus, David, Abraham, Joshua, ruth, Esther the angels, Paul, timothy all the early disciple we have to preach, teach, sing, love and be peace maker here on earth before Jesus come. Answer this question? Are we doer of God word? Are we obeying God commandment, are we? Pause and think about it before you start. This ministry is a doing ministry not just word spoken but doing all my reader action ministry, the apostle James say be ye doer of the word not hearer only deceiving your own selves for if you hear the word and don't do the word you are deceiving yourself read James 1:22 and 23. I would implore all the reader if you don't know Jesus as your lord and savior let Jesus come in your heart and accept him as the only savior that can save your soul: roman 10:10 states written by the apostle Paul: for with the heart man believe unto righteousness and with the mouth confession is made unto salvation; whosoever believe on Jesus shall be save.

The people were pigeon meaning they were ashamed and believe all thing are possible when you truly believe with your heart. Our job as believers is to share God message with family, friends, co-worker, stranger and invite them to the house of God. We need to hear this welcome flag from Jesus *welcome home my faithful children you have pass the test that I set for you all* some people including family, friend and coworker will never welcome you but Jesus will welcome you for who you are no merit with Jesus you are a part of the welcome team Jesus love you for who you are not for what he can get from you like the world love you because you are famous and have money that not love is infatuation meaning wrong kind of love but good news have Jesus unconditioned agape love good or bad, rich or poor Jesus love you my friends receive Jesus love in your heart, mind and soul next chapter will be about love and prayer we getting deep so you can know what real life is all about.

Holy Spirit Blessing and Benefits

The fruit of the holy spirit is indeed blessing, favor, promotion and increase good health when we obey, father Abraham was from different country name the Chaldees these pigeon people never believe in God but Abraham and his family believe in Jesus and serve Jesus, God appear to Abraham tell him leave your country and come let me show you a land where I will give you, Abraham could have say no I am not going because is whole life was with Chaldees but he obey and go where God tell him. When he and is family start travelling God was leading him to the new land yes, he arrives he and his family God start to bless him more than what he did have before here how apostle James sum up about Abraham believe God and it was imputed unto him for righteousness and God call his friend because of Abraham obedient and relationship with God he was bless. Are we having a relationship with God, are we have religion and tradition? Relationship and the spirit take us to Jesus himself. When Jesus was on earth his own people never know him because of their religious believe only who did have a relationship know Jesus even until now only brethren with relationship know Jesus and have the true spirit. I encourage you all my reader get a relationship with Jesus not ritual and tradition or religion, read the bible ask Jesus for wisdom, knowledge and understanding of the holy spirit like king Solomon that ask God for wisdom knowledge and understanding to rule Israel of course God give him all he ask for, be careful what you ask Jesus for, I remember couple year I was in Florida and I was at gas station getting some coffee and young man say to me pray for him and I ask what should I pray for he says *pray that God give me strength* only few people ask to pray for the things that can give them material until present I still pray for that young man God bring to my mind all the time and is over 3 year feed at Jesus and the holy spiritual table every day you will be bless immensely. Settle down and get to know who is Jesus just going to the house of God or few hours per day can't let you know who this Jesus is, but quality time spent with him like when you studying your book to be somebody great dedication and maturity or spending time with family and friends. I am preaching all over the world 2021 I preach in over ten (10) state in the USA to God be the glory great thing he has done thank Jesus he chose me Claudia, I was calling around for cheap ticket to go to England for 2022 summer because I lady I know gone to France last December 2021 I was taken up in the moment want to go on January 16, 2022 God gave me a dream seeing myself in the country of Canada I can clearly seeing a man in the dream give me some money I wake up and journal it into my book, and start to look up all my friends in Canada yes I call one of them she say you can use my car when you get there so you see some dream or true in the dream I see the man giving me so money when I wake and call my friend in Canada right away she say come I have a car for you to drive and somewhere for you to stay that God providing for us to do is work, so place I preach God send people to pay my hotel fee, give me money food and other thing that keep us going thank you Jesus someone out there tell the master thank because if it was God on her side we would number amongst the dead but the song say he kept amen. Aren't God good yes, he is my fan and friends Jesus speak to us in dream, true the word of God, true prophets, pastor and who he chose to give is information, Jesus will come and speak to you himself spoken word are we obeying Jesus I do, read the book of Daniel most of the time he spoke to Daniel some of is preacher true dream. The key in the kingdom of God is obeying, believe, praying, faith, the holy spirit, read God word, feast at God table every day. Apply Jesus in our socially life, physical life, mental life, private life and spiritually life simple pray before you go out, seek God before you get marry, seek him before you get, I job, buy a house and for your friends, may sure we put Jesus first. The holy spirit keep us grounded and strong genesis 13:2 states Abraham was more wealthy in cattle, silver and gold because he obey God the priest name Melchizedek he was the king of Salem meet Abraham and he bless him with tithes and offering when God tell Abraham to sacrifice is son Isaac he was going to and when God see the obeying Abraham he stop him saying now for sure I know you love me Abraham obedient in action not rebellion, first he leave his country and the second time he test his faith to sacrifice his son, he won God command, make sure you win with God not man.

The spirit gives us when we seek for a word, a song and a prophecy don't take it on yourself to do it on your own we will fail big time, some time when I am going to minister if the holy spirit don't give a word, I cancel i just don't want to look foolish and ashamed Jesus must go before us in everything we do and speak. Like king Saul disobey God, and the enemies kill him the power of the holy spirit left him, samson the strongest man in the bible disobey God and the enemies take him out the spirit left him. We must rely on Jesus and the spirit to be our guiding light before we do anything in the kingdom of God and the search light. I see lot of temples close down Christians miss place because people taking on them self to do it on their own of course they fail because it was not base on God it was self-righteous movement. When I was in Boston state in the USA, I met a young man he told me is wife is trying to start a church in Africa, the first thing I ask her did God tell you to start the church she says yes, I told him Jesus will provide everything you need to start. Because a lot of us following people to do thing and it not what God want for you, why not ask Jesus, he will tell you just like how he switches my destination on me the nick of time. Apostle Paul was chosen of God to preach is word he was preaching to the Corinth church he tell them I came not to you with excellent of speech of men, but the wisdom of God, declaring unto you the testimony of God my speech and preaching was not with enticing word of man wisdom but in demonstration of the spirit and power of God, which none of the prince of this world knew for if they know it, they would not have crucified the lord Jesus of glory, let the word of our mouth be in line with the holy spirit. Rely on the spirit of God like a baby that suck the mother breast for milk apply the same rule in the kingdom of God okay, but God reveal them to us is chosen servant. For us to know the mystery of God we have to have the spirit of Jesus not the false spirit. The important of the spirit before Jesus go back to his father God, he says to the 11 apostles don't go to preach nowhere until you receive the infilling of the holy spirit Jesus tell them john truly baptized with water but I Jesus will baptize with holy ghost not many days hence. Jesus depart to his father and they were praying to receive the holy ghost they were sitting down not doing nothing they were on one accord praising God and praying to receive the seal of approval act 2:1 to 3 and when the day of Pentecost was fully come they were all with one accord in one place there is great power in unity the devil can't break unity guess what *suddenly there came a sound from heaven as of a rushing mighty wind and it fill the place where they were praying every one of them receive the holy spirit 1. Because of the unity bond 2. Because they were worshiping and pray, they put work and expectation to your waiting yes, they got it and you can get it too. To maintain the holy spirit, we must pray and call it in every day it needs to be fresh like a drink of water make sure it properly activated so we can be powerful, step out in faith, put work to get what you need from Jesus be bold, courageous, be passionate let faith arise in what we are doing have the zeal of God. Look at some preacher and singer watch and listen to their song the joy, the happiness, the spirit fill those preaching and song when they are finish we don't want to leave that the afterward of the spirit you know it from God, like singer sister Scully, grace thriller, Tasha cobb, Kim walker smith, CeCe winner, Hezekiah walker people always say to me sister Claudia I was bless by your preaching I tell them is not me is the holy spirit of God not taking credit I give it where it belong glory to the one that send us *Jesus*.

We are the church not the building our body: so, we must house the spirit in our body, the bible says my kingdom come here on earth we have a responsibility to let people see Jesus true us by sharing the word, giving, sharing and loving each other. 1 Corinth 3:16 the kingdom of God filters not in word but in power and the holy spirit of operation and meekness. For example, some work place run on operation and production so their client can get the product for the company to stay in business they have to produce. For God kingdom to stay in operation stay alive here on earth we must have the holy spirit alive in our mind, soul and heart to achieve all is goal when we go witness and preach, we produce soul, healing and deliverance people getting prosperous we must produce good fruit in the kingdom of God be a super producer for Jesus, when you go to this work place every month some coworker is the super producer of the month because of hard work be God super produce amen and amen.

The spirit promote: we are giving you the different side of the holy spirit the spirit yes it promote you in an extraordinary way where education cant and money and fame, I want to give you the apostle joseph was the son of the Jacob that Abraham grandson Jacob have 11 more children the originally tribe of Israel but Jacob love joseph so did God love joseph, his brother was jealous of joseph his father make him beautiful coat and they envy grow more between his brother, so all of them went to feed his father sheep and the brothers throw him in a pit to die, God was with him some stranger found joseph name the midinettes they hear him cry for help rescue him God right now is rescue you out there you pain is over, your low self-esteem is over, your complain is over shout thank you Jesus the one that help joseph when they take him out of the pit, they sold him to the Ishmaelites for money they brought joseph to Egypt, God was with during all his trial one of the most famous and wealthy man bring home joseph with him name pharaoh God get joseph at place of influence and power everything joseph put his hand too was very prosperous the master saw that God was with him big time God allow the master to extend grace to joseph from be abandon slave to overseer pharaoh house and overall he have you blessing is here all my reader I feel as I write stop read and thank Jesus, what a favor God gave joseph and blessing it was heavy on joseph. Joseph trail continue when the master wife pharaoh wife love joseph and ask joseph to lie with her, joseph tell her know I will not do such thing she was upset with joseph she tell lie that joseph rape her and they believe her joseph was arrested for a crime he never do, all my reader can relate to this story of false arrest doing something you never done don't worry pray you way out Jesus is our defender and official judge but God was still with joseph in all these trail, in prison they make him take care of the other inmate even in a place of confinement he was promote Jesus process is different from manual process it unusual talking about the spirit of promotion, it does matter where you are God still can promote you not the boss or supervisor but Jesus himself will give it to you okay be optimistic and stay positive even when it don't look like it going to happen keep believing,. God was teaching joseph responsibility greater and higher promotion coming for joseph and for you to don't give up joseph story will encourage you to press on, so the master pharaoh have a dream none of his worker could interpret the dream someone tell pharaoh about joseph could interpret the dream, he tell them go get joseph out of the prison and bring him to me, when joseph arrive pharaoh tell him the dream and right away the spirit of God in joseph interpret pharaoh dream, when pharaoh see joseph interpret the dream, he say in the present of all his worker and people genesis 41:37 to 43 the thing was good in the eyes of all the servant can we find such a one as this joseph he is man that the spirit of God dwell in, no one more discreet and wise as you joseph. What a recommendation from the master to a prisoner to be abandon lie on right away pharaoh release joseph from jail and put him in charge of the whole Egypt and pharaoh take of his ring put it on joseph finger with fine linen and gold chain around his neck honor continue and make joseph to ride in the second chariot and they bow to joseph, they make him ruler over all the land of Egypt, God super spirit rock, elevate indeed promote. Joseph is a perfect example of a lot of people story you been true a lot in your life sickness, poverty, relationship problem, rejection, abandon like joseph and the list go on don't give up like joseph stay focus, build your relationship in Jesus weeping may endure for a night but joy cometh in the morning be encourage true these true life giving story I come to tell you it will happen for you too, have a bad pass God getting ready to expunge that record, low self-esteem, be talk about you are next in line for you blessing believe and receive your blessing don't give up all joseph trails he never give up God put him straight on top amen.

The spirit that lead: our next promoted apostle is Moses he was born to a Jewish mother but at the time they want to kill all male child but his mother hide Moses and put him at the edge of river in a cot but again next the master daughter saw the baby Moses she was at the river when she saw the baby Moses he was a proper child and she take the baby Moses and bring him home and ask Moses mother to nurse the baby for her, she never know she was the real mother of Moses. Moses grows up in one of wealthiest home in Egypt and got good first-class education there, when Moses grows in an adult stage, he realizes he was a Jewish son when he sees the Egyptian fighting the Jewish people, he was upside and retaliate back. Finally, Moses left their house and flea to a different county and find a lady and married. The call to lead he was at the backside of the mountain feeding his father law sheep when the angel of the lord appears to him in flame of fire in the midst of bush say *Moses, Moses and of course Moses' answer say God hear I am God say take of your shoe because the place where you stand his holy ground my brother and sister take of sin, take of pride, take off revenge God himself need to bless you right now like Moses obey. God identify himself to Moses God want to identify himself to you are you listening, he says I am the God of our father the God of Abraham, God of Isaac and the God of Jacob, and Moses hide his face he was afraid to look on God come face to face with the living God confront all your enemies too and friends. You would ask why God chose Moses because he see meekness, he see leadership, he see obedient and clean heart again God business is not like the world and how people see you, someone never give you the job because they think you are not capable of doing a good job but God send for you because he see that you are capable to work but he even go far and give more favor and more benefit and very good salary than what the first boss was offering you mysterious God. God tell Moses he needs him to go back to Egypt where he flew from to liberate and the children of Israel from the cold bondage they were in slave in Egypt, Moses and Aaron go and lead the children of Israel from the wicked hand of pharaoh. We are free until present walk, talk free no more chains over us our father martin Luther king say it not the skin but content and character that matter we miner in the major and major in the miner Jesus look in the heart big time that how he promote his people, the bible say Moses was the most humbleness meekest man alive he was a praying apostle fill with holy spirit on fire, he also the only apostle speak to God face to face when he was with the people he have to wear a vale what a blessing when you are chosen from God himself no pastor or member chose you but the most high God chose us. I remember over 20 year I was at my work place when I hear the thunder rolling voice say daughter that not where I want you to serve, I need you to go on the high way and bye way and preach my word, guess who was that voice Jesus himself came for me like Moses call until present 2022 I can tell you I am very humble and honor to know the great God come for me himself glory to your name Jesus many are call but only few are chosen I can tell you I am chosen big time until I come face to face with the living God. When I was in the state of Connecticut Jesus take me to a house in the spirit and say bless these family my mind keeps blowing until present that why I call in the spirit every single day do the same all who read this holy book a word from the wise I am still hearing the voice and see Jesus' face to face. 2021 of November I was coming from New York when I stop the car in the state of Georgia, I spent couple day there preaching and giving out tracks as I sit in the car, I hear the same voice that call me over 20 year says *daughter don't worry the devil his defeated* plain as day I journal it always records what Jesus tell just like how you journal your life story. Of course the devil is defeat treat him like one by saying know to evil and wickless that defeated the devil., couple year I was in New York a awake about 4 am when I was in worship that same voice talking and I see Jesus in person all over me, i was sitting in my car in Kendal Miami about 2pm in the after Jesus himself appear to me in person he spoke to me and he came with a big umbrella that an arrange and confirmation from Jesus the try to steal my car it never work, they rob me it never work it a living prove that for sure we are cover and protect by the most high God we are safe my friends saying daughter you are well protected when you are in God, Jesus spirit will show you Jesus in person and you will hear is voice Jesus say my sheep hear my voice and know for sure is me Jesus just like you know you family voice and your pastor or friends we need to be quiet to hear his voice turn of tv and radio and social media time for everything okay if you have to go somewhere quiet especially if you have a busy house, the women would wake 4am in the morning and drive at a spot just to meet Jesus and hear his voice that commitment in the first degree make time like us and this young lady and stop saying I am busy and I don't have time make time it call time management and priority. Take a praise break and praise him like these early Christian and the angels Exodus 12:29 song of freedom sing a song of praise for your salvation, your healing, your deliverance, your prosperity, your peace, love and joy stop read and pause and: praise God just worship praise God for all his goodness on your life and family the wall was torn down because of praise, David praise God and win the enemy, Josaphat praise God and slew the enemies, Gideon praise God and defeat the enemies so do the same is our weapon as believer use it and fight the enemies off your back right now I am experiencing peace because I pray and praise God a lot and getting favor and increase every day because of Jesus benefit for us go get it and stop waiting. Even if you don't have family, we and Jesus is your family the bible say if you are God children, we are family spiritual and biologically that okay.

The Lord speak face to face: the spirit of wisdom, knowledge and understanding allow Moses to fast and pray 40 day and night and write the commandment, God choose Aaron and his sons to minister in the priest office they make special garment for beauty and glory to entertain the spirit to have the spirit is one but we have to maintain the spirit meaning heart must be clean, we must obey what the spirit tell you to do. Moses speaks unto all that are wise hearted this is key not just beauty but all who God call he fill with power of the holy ghost and purging, consecration we are special kind of people anoint with God holy oil and favor. The oil represent the blood of Jesus if you watch me preach I always have olive oil that God have me to use and share it with those who want to use it read psalm 23:5, psalm 92:10 and number, Leviticus all over the bible you see the special use of the olive oil, as you continue to read this book I show you different thing God use to bring salvation to his people including water, rod and dove that represent the holy ghost when john baptize Jesus the dove was right unto of his head you going learn something from this book and the bible it very deep and interested some book I read and read over all 2 and 3 times this book going to be read more than one time it blessing, salvation and life maps restoration.

The Spirit that made: I show you the Jesus, God spirit in action that God himself have to use to created us and the whole world the spirit passes down to all who he calls and choose to do is work here on earth the spirit still connected nothing change about that, Jesus has to use the same spirit to pray, to do miracle he turns water into wine, he heals the sick and raise the dead he walks on water. So all my friend and fan and family make sure you get the right spirit so your life will be transform from normal to extra super every single day, pray for the holy spirit, pray Jesus come to my soul fresh anointed like fresh water and fruits every day not junk food, maintain nature you relationship with God make it a top priority so God can bless us in abundant you don't have to follow people and do what they do you are different the same spirit will tell you exactly what to do, sometime people say I want to be like you Claudia I respect them saying that to me but I tell them God will give you your own stuff. Exodus 31:1 to 6 God tell Moses to call Bezalel the son of uric of the tribe of Judah and I will fill him with the spirit of God in wisdom, understanding and knowledge and in all manner of workmanship they were silversmith they make gold and silver and brass and stone and carving timber the spirit of created in everything you do, faith and prayer, fasting with the holy spirit walk hand in hand race to get the holy spirit. Some time when a new phone or new shoe come on the market you see people race stand in line for hour to get the next gadgets or shoe so race to get Jesus and the holy spirit do it, the gadgets and the shoe will go sooner or later but the spirit will be with you every day again priority friends. The spirit travel because the children of Israel was traveling from Egypt to the different country but very interesting God guide them true the leader Moses but there is certain country, they want to reside so Moses send some men to spies out the land, just like us when you buying a house or car are even clothes, we are not shopping one place we looking for the best buy aren't we? When they go to spies out the land some of the men gave an evil report to Moses says there were giant living in the land but 2 men come back with God report about the same land that Caleb and Joshua tell Moses the land was good and fruitful, they have the spirit of God living in the inside they tell correct information number 14:24 but my servant Caleb because he had another spirit and have follow me fully meaning heart felt relationship he and Joshua I will bring them into the land of paradise flowing with milk and honey the rest of the men never inherit the land because of the flesh and there evil report. Those 2 eventually live in the land of paradise because of the spirit they have look at the spirit in action I make sure I give you the spirit in all is operation put the spirit at work in your personal life and ministry and work let go we must see things from God Jesus perspective not the flesh be like Caleb and Joshua excellent spirit.

Spirit of leadership continue: God choose Joshua to take over from Moses retire Moses appoint Joshua and God fill him with the holy spirit to continue to lead the children of Israel, Moses encourages Joshua be strong and courageous fear not the lord thy God that go with thee and will not fail thee nor forsake thee. Let the word of God sink in our heart that thou will meditate on God word all the days of our life. Let be not just reading the word but be doer of God word, great benefit and success and prosperity. Next important thing protects our heart with all diligence for out of it are the issues of life God promotion is from the heart. Psalm 77:6 let follow after love and desire spiritual gift love is the root to give the spirit of truth and understanding, inspiration flow to do the thing of God to lead, preach, sing and dance. 1 Corinthians 14:16 – 17 the spirit of God teach us order and respect when we brethren come together we must have psalm, doctrine, tongue and revelation let all thing be done in order to edifying of the church the spirit of the prophet are subject to the prophets God is not the author of confusion but a God of peace, it must be in all churches of the saints warning: if anyone think of himself to be a prophet or spiritual let him acknowledge that the things I write unto you are the commandment of the lord 1 Corinthians 14:37 believe is most important in the kingdom of God to receive salvation, healing, the holy spirit, faith and prosperity is a must we believe and have faith. We don't see God in person but by faith with the spirit we can see Jesus.

Important information for the believer: the different level of God glory moving higher just like in your work place from cleaning the plane to own the plane, from cleaning the floor in your work place to promoted to owning that company, is the same in the kingdom of God but Jesus give us that promotion, many are call but few are chosen. Get this in your spirit one glory to the sun, another glory of the moon another to the star so is the resurrection of the dead it sown incorruption it raise in glory it sown in dishonor it sown in natural body, it raise in the highest form our spiritual body for example before Jesus go down 3 days in the tomb he give back H the spirit but the third day God use back the spirit to raise Jesus from the dead the spirit is indeed alleviation, restoration, resurrection and life and promotion. God allow Othniel the deliverer to judge Israel but before he start his duty the spirit of the lord came upon him Othniel right away, he go out to war with the enemies and won, is like you go to school to learn how to be teacher when you left college and go for a job interview the first things they ask for is your certificate and test your skill if you can manage the work, well Jesus fill us with the holy spirit so is spiritual work will be done the qualification in the body of Christ is the holy spirit and believe obey. God right now need a mother for his people and a father he chooses prophetess Deborah and barrack the next judge of Israel and accompany her was barrack the father the enemies was defeated because of Deborah leadership and mother Jael.

Apostle Gideon job was to defeated the enemies that oppress them daily when they were in there country, the angel appear unto Gideon says *the lord is with thee thou mighty man of velour go and rescue Israel from the hand of the enemies, Gideon reply to the lord I am poor and my families is poor I am the least of my father house: just like some of us God tell you to do something you have excuse, God answer Gideon go I am with you, just like king David God was with him everywhere he was Jesus is with us don't be afraid to God assignment okay. Guess what believe Jesus is with us we could have die; we could be on the street but Jesus is with us in good time and bad time the bible says even thou we walk true the valley of the shadow of dead we fear no evil because Jesus is with us is rod and his staff comfort us is blood surely cover us and save us believe. I and my family and people I know was in great problem and Jesus rescue us from evil hand, Gideon and his people worship and blow the trumpet simple the enemies were destroying because indeed God was with them, he assures God is with you all I saw him covering us with is big umbrella rest in his promise and trust him no doubting.

God chose apostle Jephthah: this apostle a lot of reader of the bible skip Jephthah he was important like king David and king solo mom was reject by his own family because his father have him with strange women so the wife throw him out the house, some of us can relate to rejection from family, friends and co- worker. Now they were in trouble and the family send back for Jephthah, he came and said you expel me why you send back for me; they answer come and fight for us who reject you they are getting ready to call you back and God getting ready to give you a higher promotion Jephthah come back and forgive who reject him that why God use him and promote him the key here is forgive who hurt you. Because the enemies want to destroy us and our people, right away they make him captain over them. The spirit of the lord came upon Jephthah and he pass over the different country fighter for God children, he makes a vow unto the lord say let me defeat the enemies of my people yes, the enemies was defeated. Judge apply Jesus apply the holy spirit to fight for you, you family and your country don't give victory is for you okay quit is defeated pursue is winning go pursue like king David 11:29 the word of God have story like your story your trail is over like David, Jephthah and Esther.

Women God chose to work: there was a famine in Israel so Naomi and his husband and family go to a country name Moab these people worship false God, because of the famine Naomi go there, just like some of us we have a problem we gone and leave our family or walk of the job we must face our problem knowing Jesus is on our side to help us true, confront what before us don't run. Naomi 2 sons marry the women ruth was the lady marry to Naomi's son, but the 2 sons die and Naomi husband she run to a different country but face worse problem. She decided that she going back to Israel ruth tell her I am leaving my people and go back with you Naomi she did see God love on Naomi and grace we call it reel effect. When both ladies arrive ruth start work in the vineyard the owner whose name is Boaz he saw ruth and start inquire who is this young lady and they met. Ruth finds favor with the king because she works good in the vineyard are we giving God our all-meaning heart worship like David, the women that anoint Jesus before he dead she anoints and she worship a sinner women know how to worship God, are we preaching thus say the lord, are we praying faith fill prayer, are we singing holy spirit song from our heart answer your question, don't get around like judas be in it deep give it your all. I see business place that use to open on Sunday close so they worker can go to the house of God, place like chick fill a, hobby lobby and other these place always open Sunday but I know God convict the owner of these business he will convict you give God what belong to him okay. Boaz was Naomi's mother law family so ruth was in the lineage of Boaz that same linage came king David and Jesus. Boaz finally marry ruth because ruth take a step of faith and leave her county like Abraham and many of us leave our country come to America, Canada, England and Africa and you know where you are now but not in the county you were born isn't it. I can tell you blessing is coming to you big time 2022 until God come, keep pressing in all my reader keep positive, keep praising and access God tell your blessing come it coming keep your expectation high look how these chicken scratch for food this bird always looking for food keep scratch. Next women of God are Hannah did marry but was barren she pray to God to open her womb she need a baby a lot of women can relate to Hannah story God open her womb and she have a baby name Samuel and he grew and become one of the greatest prophet, lady Elizabeth and Sarah was barren too women of the bible, they pray of many year over 70 year old they have baby Elizabeth have john the baptize that baptize Jesus and sara have Isaac that have Jacob there come the tribe of Israel. Keep believing I see this couple in Africa marry for over 60 years never have a baby they just have a twin baby in 2020, we have a Jesus still working miracle people get heal from covid 19, I got heal some many times too. God will do the super natural when doctor give you over God give you a miracle believe. The lord appear unto Samuel like king Solomon for the first time in a country name shallot and introduce himself to Samuel, and encounter with the living God go and introduce yourself to who God need you to go don't be selfish, you are looking a partner go and introduce yourself to that person male can do it or female it does matter you gender : I just ask in the previous chapter when last you have encounter with Jesus Samuel did, and Samuel judge Israel all his life good to talk to minister but try hard so God himself can talk to you. The people need a king, so God tell Samuel to appoint king Saul after the appointment the spirit of the lord came in Saul and he prophesy but Saul go and disobey God and God take back the spirit don't sin against God that he has revoke back the spirit from you he takes it back from king Saul 1 Samuel 13:11 to 13. So God use prophet Samuel to go and appoint another king because Saul fail, Samuel go to family house in Israel name Jesse and out of all Jesse children God chose David ruth came from the lineage of David too and Samuel anoint David with the anointed oil in the midst of his family watch this: the spirit of God came in David from that day forward and because Jesus take back the spirit from Saul the evil spirit take over Saul, so be careful which spirit you are operating under, make sure you have the Jesus spirit. Jesus spirit in activation David with the right spirit defeat the giant, slew enemies and gangs and won and of course David fame raise over all Israel and to our now generation now I love David character and strategy how he was super humble rely on God that no prophet does be like David pattern how unique he was and lay back, Moses was the meekness apostle all of them was indeed unique you see the spirit get you famous like David. So, fail Saul invite David to his house to get rid of the evil spirit which David did Saul was still the present king and let David live in his house and learn how to be the next king like joseph have to be in Pharoah house to learn how to rule, we need to get experience to rule and be good worker, good wife, good preachers, good prayer warrior etc. The spirit of good teach David to behave himself and be wise and be humble so we can learn from Jesus the lord was with him, please spent quality time with Jesus that can give us great life. Pattern David seeking God for direction and everything, now the enemies took all David have and his men have burn there city with fire., take his family it was so bad that the people was about to stone him for the first time he experience defeat, but watch the principle David how he got back victory: he go to the priest and borrow the ephod the high priest ceremonial garment then he pray to God because he know he cannot fight unless God is with him in the prayer he ask God what shall I do the enemies take everything I have: God answer David say pursue after the enemies we shall recover, is God talking to you to go get back your family, go get back your job, go get back your ministry God gave you anything the enemies stole from you go get it back like David but pray before you go seek God direction on it. 1 Samuel 30:7 to 8 David recover everything the enemies stole including getting back his families. We are fighting in prayer, worship and reading God word and living holy in obeying God command your family coming back home, you getting miracle money, as for you and your family God salvation is your, our shame shall turn into victory, we will be God rose garden spreading all over the world, we shall be the head and not the tail, as I Claudia Gods end time prophet write this manuscript I see restoration, I see the loss coming home, I see blessing in an unusual setting, I see promotion operantly I see God children ruling the world because of holiness, position yourself for a takeover of Jesus: pause and say thank you Jesus praise God for your victory it your Jesus go to the cruel cross he shed his precious blood that the devil could not touch, the angel themselves bring Jesus blood back to heaven the devil cannot touch you and your family because the same blood cover us like the children of Israel in Egypt believe we have the victory. Amen

The 2 prophets were Elijah and Elisha: Elijah was the most popular prophet in the bible even until now he obeys God big time with the spirit of God get revelation about what was going to happen before it happens real Christian should be getting revelation if you connect to the holy spirit and Jesus are you getting revelation and hearing from God answer this question? 2017 I was in New York doing mission preaching, Jesus appears to me in a vision just like Daniel and Solomon, he put me on pedals stone and show me the whole world tearing apart tree dropping, house and car dropping and people when I see Jesus, he says daughter * these people evil and sin his too much* I start to warn and preach all over New York what God was saying, like when Noah and Jonah were warning backslidden Israel. I preach my heart out and preach on social media. From 2017 now is 2022 virus, plane crash , tornado, fire, shooting and poverty, just got fire in 2021 December in Denver Colorado, 2021 flooding in New York, tornado in Kentucky, fire in California disaster all over the world, the virus start in China and Africa, we see raising crime all over the world like never before, we see democracy in America was in trouble, we see angry supporter march on the white house to avert the law of justice, we see present Ukraine want to fight with Russia, right now pentagon put troop on the alert as NATO boosts eastern Europe presence, we see lot of positive case of virus, right now in the USA California burning down in 2022 right now we are experiencing economy is at a crossroad, China and America in a trade war. My advice to all those who take time to read this timely book the solution is giving Jesus your heart, mind and soul turn from our evil ways and start doing things God way, be the solution and not a part of the problem. So, Elijah was so much fill with God spirit that he goes to heaven alive read 2 kings 2 all of us must continue to take over the mantle not just Elisha but us that call on Jesus Elisha take over the mantle Elijah leave.

Jesus the world messiah the greatest flow of the holy spirit from conception to delivery God choose the peasant lady Mary a virgin to give birth to a king and savior of us all, Mary word was my soul magnify the lord and my spirit praise his name the mother of Jesus was a worshipper before she was favor to bring in the Messiah, God chose his people base on who there were before they were chosen of God, he is not going to choose fool and hater not at all. That an honor and favor God chose Mary hear how the written of Matthew put it *now the birth of Jesus Christ was on this wise when his mother Mary was espoused to joseph before they came together she was found with a child the seed was *the holy ghost* look at the holy spirit conception different part of the holy spirit in previous chapter I show the created holy spirit, I show you the working holy spirit, I show you the promotion side of the holy spirit, the wisdom and knowledge of the holy spirit, the favor of the holy spirit and now I showing you the conception of the holy spirit, the bible say from you were in your mother womb I knew you before you came out of our mother womb I sanctified you to be a messiah like Jesus, a pastor, a bishop, a prayer warrior, a singer and giver, a leader, a mentor, a lover, peacemaking put in the purpose God have you hear to do? ... And do it. God show his prophet Jesus before he was born the prophet Isaiah saw Jesus high and lifted up and his trail fill the temple, if you are Intune to the spirit and Jesus he will tell you thing before it happen just like your family and friend tell their secret that how God do it but with Jesus you see it before it happen it name spirit of discernment every believe should have this gift like the holy spirit gift, even the name of Jesus the mother Mary never chose but God tell Mary the name the baby *Jesus* meaning salvation. When Jesus grows into maturity, he went to the baptizer to get baptize and the apostle john baptize Jesus and the dove that represent the holy spirit fell on Jesus' head and the holy spirit increase in Jesus we have to come to a place in God that we need all of the holy spirit and all of Jesus fully we must decrease and Jesus must increase that we rely on Jesus to make our decision. With the holy spirit Jesus go in the wilderness and fasted and pray 40 days and 40 nights just like apostle Moses that pray 40 days and 40 night to know God more and write the commandment in exodus 20 we produce good fruit that the end product of the holy spirit it let you shine anywhere you go you always have work, almost when I am going to work for Jesus I say Jesus what should and do this particular day and the Jesus and the spirit tell what to do and where to go I side of the holy spirit it give us clear direction. If we are God children we pray and fast regularly., Jesus was tempted of the devil like all of us some time we feel to steal, gossip and do evil but like Jesus say no to the devil don't let him trick you and then you are sorry. Jesus was victorious the devil left him and Jesus go to Nazareth and different place preaching God word that the purpose of Jesus to deliver God word to the loss and dying heal the sick, raise the dead and help the poor his fame quickly spread all over the world until rise and shine my brother and sister get stand up and let your voice be heard and your vote anywhere you go in the world some Christian think we should not vote but Jesus instruct us give to Cesar what due to him including vote, paying your taxes and don't owe any one, the holy spirit give us mercy and grace like you going to see the judge the spirit is present to tell us what to say the bible say when Jesus was before is accuser he never talk until the spirit give him a word lean on Jesus not on you own ability you will fail and the angel come down and strengthen him present your all on the altar and surrender to the one that will help you. Sometime God I to let you go through the trail Jesus is love son go through it, job is dearest go true it there when time David go through it and he say my body is so heavy but God let him go through it. I personally been through a lot rejection of family and friends, homeless, betrayal of believer big time, the talk about me for nothing but I learn to pray and lean on Jesus on changing hand Emmanuel God with us never leave us he hold us through the trial stop act and talk defeat we won because Jesus is with us okay in Matthew 9:37 and 38 Jesus say to his disciple the harvest is truly plenteous but the laborer's are few let pray that people can come and work for Jesus preach his work, teach and work in his vineyard ruth work for Jesus I was retore fully God gave her next husband, Jesus declare when he go in temple they give him the book of the law and he read says the work place call it manifesto or in politics we Christian call it the covenant that is whole purpose *the spirit of the lord God is upon me Jesus because he anointed me to preach good tidings unto to meek he sent me to bind up the broken hearted, to proclaim liberty to the captive and the open of the prison to them that are bound to proclaim the acceptable year of the lord and the day of vengeance of our God to comfort all they that mourn to give us beauty for ashes then the oil of joy for mourning the garment of praise for the spirit of heaviness, that they might be call the tree of righteousness the planting of the lord that he will be glorified. That all who are call of God to do so let us do it, next instruction from Jesus, he tell us *go ye therefore into the highways and as many as ye shall find bid them to the marriage so we go and witness God word lets share God word we are in the last day if you want to be a part of what we are doing don't hesitate call the number anywhere you are 754 368 9454 or 1888 731 1000 let continue to obey God. * Jesus arrives here in a virgin womb and exit out in new tomb and make alive on the third day early morning in the first fresh air* is this amazing. We need a fresh start with God and him alone big time in a relationship style so we are to pray to Jesus who must be our shepherd, pastor and prophet, mentor. There is fake one around too but if you pray Jesus will show you the real one, many are call but few are chosen. When you have the right spirit of God you preach and teach the word from a spirit knowledge not from the flesh so the word is pass on to believer and sinner effectively so they will response positively and be save, heal, deliver and set free without you even start pray that the power of the holy spirit faith, bold prayer this women daughter was sick and she came to Jesus say master my child is sick at home the child never present but watch this the women believe the word Jesus spoke and her daughter was completely heal that women was not even a Christian but she was desperate for her daughter to get better and she did, so don't just read the book or the bible but believe for what you are praying for just a prayer away even if the person you are praying in Peru, Haiti, Jamaica, USA, Europe just put faith to your prayer with the spirit to transfer it, do it now pause and start pray and then start read back again. When Jesus was preaching and teaching all over the different country including Israel the people response with acceptance and acknowledgement some reply I have never hear the word like that Jesus speak with power and authority and with the holy spirit in him. Jesus was more famous for preaching the love of God and peace he said in all of his message love one another and love hang all the false believers because our heavenly father is love so make sure you have God love in our heart, Jesus say in his message *howbeit when the spirit of truth come he will guide us in all truth for he shall not speak of himself but whatsoever he shall he speak and he show us the thing to come until today he still showing us thing that will happen before he come., when Jesus was on the cross he said to God I give back your spirit to you God it finish man redemption have be paid that Jesus finally word the work he came here to do what complete, some of us like to do unfinish job stop at the side of the road, stop cooking, stop working and you never finish stop preaching and you never finish God work but our king finish it yes it was so bloody and painfully but he finish it with a bang, I writing but I feel like I am on a big stage preaching that the passion of the holy spirit I am enjoying writing this book so you can get the juice of it. Jesus could not give God back the spirit when he was on earth because that what he uses to accomplish God work. Most interested before he goes back to his father, he say to 11 disciples don't go preach my word until you receive the holy spirit when Jesus ascend to his father apostle peter and the 11 disciple was praying and praising God in unity guess who appear in that prayer meeting the rushing of the holy spirit and every one of them was fill with the special holy spirit and speaking in cloven tongues. When Moses was sick and tired God tell Moses get some man and prepare for me and bring them the next day, I will fill them with the spirit that on you Moses and let them continue to help you and 2 of the men that was not chosen get the holy spirit because they were near where the spirit fall look at that you may not prepare but God will still give you what you don't work for and deserve because of his mercy he give it to you. Act 2:1 to 7 when they receive the holy spirit they go out and preach God word and over three thousand people receive Jesus as their lord and savior. There was pastor right here in the USA go to a Muslim country to preach only God and the spirit can let you go in the devil zone and preach most of these people worship ala false God guess what a lot of the Muslim population leave there false God and right now start serving Jesus because of the holy spirit preacher that the spirit in operation is not the preacher is the God spirit in him do the job, I met a man in new York in the summer of 2021 giving me is testimony, he say I use to worship false God it was so bad no job I was down big time and some body introduce him to Jesus, right now he have a lot of job and prospering and of course serving the true savior Jesus so leave the false God and come to the real one that can save your soul *Jesus.* so every believer you see what grow church obedient, relationship and the holy spirit grow churches. The holy spirit was so strong on the disciple that there was a man name Simon use sorcery to bewitched the people but when evangelize Phillip go to the city with God spirit the false spirit that Simon have surrender to God servant Phillip and he receive Jesus as lord and savior just like the preacher that go to the devil zone and preach and they surrender. Right now arm yourself with God spirit that when you encounter demonic spirit they will surrender to God like Simon the witchcraft worker, they drug man will bow to God and the prostitute, the liar, the thief, the murder, the palm reader, psychic, all evil will bow greater is he that in us that he that in the world, we are more than conqueror true Christ that give us strength, we can do all thing when Jesus live in our heart, mind and soul keep focus on the prize that Jesus don't be distracted. Praise and worship Jesus that alone knock out the devil let him always be an unwelcome guest kick this devil to the curve the next weapon live holy, be silent when he is around plea the blood of Jesus on him stay alert the battle Jesus won on the cross victory thank Jesus for your victory praise is holy name./.

The spirit that build: I giving you 3 priest the lord chosen to rebuild holiness back in the kingdom of God first one Joel was call to get back backslidden Israel back to God they backslide and start sin against God so Joel job is to preach the repentance message to them just like how we are call to preach to people all over the world presently, first of all Joel call a prayer and fasting service starting gird yourself and lament ye priest and people minister come let us lie all night in sackcloth prayer and fasting that what they mean before the lord because it was disaster take over like now in the world turn ye to me people with all our heart rend your heart and not your garments return unto the lord our God and repent make sure we changing and serve God he still calling repent the lord answer Joel prayer. Say you all shall know that I am God my people shall never be ashamed *it shall come to pass that I God will pour out my spirit on all flesh we shall dream continually., I God will show wonder in heaven and earth blood and fire and pillars of smoke.* so I am calling you as an apostle of God start serving Jesus return to your first love remember where go take you from the drug den, from prison, from pride, from poverty just remember and start be holy because God is holy. Amos God calls to speak to stubborn Israel return to God and serve him., prophet Micah was call and chosen of God to warn the sinful people the prophecy saying o thou that are name the house of Jacobs is the spirit of the lord strengthen are we doing God words do good to him that walketh rightly. Prophet Micah warns the people thus said the lord concerning the false prophet that make my people to sin that bite with their teeth and cry peace and then hide and war they shall be ashamed and expose. True prophets speak the truth we are full of power by the spirit of our lord and savior Jesus Christ. Micah continues to teach says arise and thresh oh he people of Zion I make thy horn iron and thou shall beat in pieces we will be consecrate their gain unto the lord, and their substance unto the lord of the whole earth. Prophet Habakkuk God chose to preach to is people he preaches repentance message to God children; the word of Habakkuk says *write the vision make it plain and act it run with it* do we all is the continuation of these prophets and preacher yes, we are continuing to run with the vision God gave us. Prophet Haggai chosen of God to free the children of Israel from Babylonian jail and build God house go up to the mountain and bring material I will take pleasure in it I will be glorified say the lord of host one more time the spirit of building and recreation. Priest Ezra was chosen of God to restore Israel from is ruin he say rise up the chief of our father of Judah and Benjamin and the priest and Levites with all them whose spirit God raise to go build the house of the lord everyone in the body of Christ God give us different gifts and talent, as give these preacher Jesus give different assignment to build, to preach, to prophesy it unique gifting., Nehemiah was God chosen builder he also build the torn down wall of Jerusalem and it was build all the enemies that was trying to stop the wall God defeat them so you know God give you a project to do and people come against you like Nehemiah continue to do it. I was in my community hearing shot ringing out but when I look I see a man get shot but he never give up even thou he was down he was fighting that the spirit believer need even when the attach coming keep fighting back in prayer, praise and reading God word bottom line don't give up like that young man, like a solider on the battle field, like a warrior that never give up thou homeless, thou sickness, thou be alone, thou lose everything bottom line never give up be encourage it Abraham Lincoln go 8 time for the presidency but the last time he won I mean yes 8 time never give up be encourage all my reader and buy this book and give to someone to read or for a present that real stuff., because we talking president we see the democracy change in America and all over the world that we were bless to have our first black president barrack Obama that the dream martin Luther king have and that what God mean in the bible when Jesus say not the outside appearance but the heart no body must be treated like nothing because of the color of their skin, or because of their status or where they come from it not for me and God and many people around the world I am saying everyone must be respected, I personal come under racism but learn to forgive these hater and pray Jesus to help them and save them I calling on all of you forgive who hurt in some way or another be polite about it too okay let move on.

Apostle Paul God chosen man: before he was Paul is first name was Saul a false Christian was going around killing Christian and putting them in jail, just like some of us we baptize we say we are Christian but we hide and do evil that what Saul was doing. Until he has an encounter with Jesus when he was going to persecute the Christian God lick Saul of the horse and said Saul why persecutes thou me it not my people it me Jesus, you think you are fighting against us but its God I see people coming against us for nothing some pass and some suffering because we are innocence. And he was down blind for 3 days until God send is servant to pray for him and heal his blindness and God fill him with the holy ghost. But before he gets the holy spirit

God blind him some of us if we don't stop sin like Saul, he is getting ready to blind us don't let God wrath catch you it dangerous so start serve Jesus and please do good this is the last day we are living in, thereafter he start preaching God word and he change is name to apostle Paul. You see some name we have we need to change it and change our nature and behavior to0, Paul name change he was restoring both in name and character brand new man in Christ so we are transforming when we have Jesus and the holy spirit living in our heart, don't let know body put you back in the pass tell them Jesus' blood change me into a brand-new man and women and you are well change like Saul to Paul amen. I hear a lady give her testimony at the house of the lord say she use to work at the bank and she stole some money she does her time in jail but when she gets out, they're employ her back that how God forgive us just like that boss isn't God good my friend yes God is super good. That my word. Apostle Paul writes most of the New Testament with the wisdom, knowledge and understanding of Jesus and the holy spirit he witnesses all over the world to everyone God send him to, I personally have a Jesus and Paul ministry we are travelling preacher in city, country, temple, bus and train just simple walking and sharing God word it does not matter your location even if it's one shares the word the bible says when one come to the lord heavenly rejoice amen. What Jesus call you to do answer this question?... And let us know we can help you fulfil what is that calling on your life you must know what Jesus tell you to do. When he calls Paul, he tells him what he should do, when Jesus calls me, Claudia the author of this book he specifically tells me what to do he said go in the highway and byways and witness to my people this what I do for over 26 year and more. When the boss or supervisor give you a job they tell how they want the job to be done don't it, what I realize when Paul preach in all the places he never left these people until they receive the infilling of the holy ghost., are we preaching and teaching the holy ghost to our members, we need to read the bible with the knowledge of the holy spirit you see as believer we must have the holy ghost to see and know Jesus and to do is work here on earth from genesis to revelation is the holy spirit so we cannot do nothing in the kingdom of God until you have that holy spirit if you going to bible school make sure they teach you the holy spirit okay the same apostle Paul was theologian was educated at the best school back in Israel and yet he was going around persecuting Christian until God change him and right now he is changing you from a false Christian to the real one let me ask you do you want to change?..... Answer change is right here Paul want to change and indeed he change. The proof is in the word of God read the word, when you buy a television, you see they have a book that tell you how to operate the television the manual well applies the same rule in God, he gave us a manual name the holy bible read it and study the word. The discernment of the holy spirit it was God prophets from all over the one Agabus signified by the spirit say there is great famine that should hit the world it came to pass when something going to happen the spirit show us before it happens it call the spirit of truth correct information. The bible says if prophets prophesy it must come to pass if its truth. The spirit heavy on Paul that everywhere he preach the church of God grow in number from a nations to a perfect man of God the bible say he caught up in the third heaven he is where God is we have the first heaven, the second heaven and the third heaven Paul highly promoted looking forward to me him and our lord and savior Jesus Christ and all the man and women of God and looking forward to see you there so live for Jesus in holiness, when I was on the road preaching I think it was in Louisiana state Jesus show me I dream see some of the apostle in white like they were doing a photo shoot the spirit in me let me see these things I am so honor to see. But when the false believer see it they were fill with envy and jealous and come against Paul but God is with us all don't worry Jesus is with us on November 2021 when I was in George state, Jesus say with a loud voice daughter don't worry the devil is defeated I mention it again so you know don't worry we have the victory in Jesus, so my brother and sister don't worry Jesus is with you all, when Paul was leaving there city he shook the dust of his feet against them as testimony do the same sometime when we go witness people slam there door in our face, stone us but do like Paul dust the dust of your feet and go don't force no body to know Jesus they have to make their choice. So, when the disciple left, they were rejoicing and carry the holy ghost we are carrier of the holy spirit and is presence that good way to exit, God which know our heart bare witness giving us the holy ghost even as he did unto us put no different between, we and them he purified our heart by faith. The ordination of elders and apostle by Paul that the motivation of the establishment of church in faith and the churches increase because of the holy spirit, if your church is not increasing search yourself if you doing it Jesus' way or your way make sure its God way are you seeing an increase in your temple? Answer it you and God now. I been in churches all over the world some increase and some do not the truth of the matter is not our way is God way let go and let God and spirit will tell what to do, just like you have a job you cannot work until the boss tell you what to do you have to please your boss don't it: when I was working in the work place some rule still stand for me for instance I like to record especially when Jesus speak to me, I still like to wake up early like when I was going to work, I still like to listen to God like listening to somebody talking to me, apply the same rule in God kingdom don't it: apply the same rule in God kingdom. Paul gets a vision from God where to go and preach he was not planning to go that route but Jesus says this is where I want you to go and he obey and go acts 16:9 Paul say *Paul vision there stood a man of Macedonia and pray him saying come over to Macedonia and help us, I am giving you an invitation come and help us build God kingdom here on earth before he come. The bible says don't build on other foundation go where you are sent by the one that paid his life for this church *Jesus* it means if someone have clothes shop you don't want to start a clothes shop beside that person shop, so God will tell where to build the house of the lord, where to go and witness he has our final destination seek him for direction. So, Paul was in another city and see some believer in Jesus and he ask them do you receive the holy spirit they say no but look at a true man of God Paul lay his hand on them and pray for them and they receive the infilling of the holy spirit. We are introducing the holy spirit to the global body of Christ I read a book of minister that write it he was Baptist before he converted to Christian but he knows he need that holy spirit and he tarry and get the holy spirit when he goes to the church where he pastor, he introduces the holy spirit to them some believe and get and some don't we have to want the spirit to get it. Tarry until you get the holy spirit read acts 19:2 to 7, he prays for the sick this time he uses handkerchiefs different thing God use to bring healing and salvation like Jesus and other disciple and everyone was healed, and they bring gift to Paul and the other disciples the people see the spirit in Paul how he preaches and heal the sick and the people shower him with gift. So, you don't have to beg when people see Jesus and the holy spirit in you, they will give you without you begging. You sew a nice dress and when you wear the dress people just say I like that dress tell me where you buy it, I need one like that one. That how people see the holy spirit in you I am bringing real like story so you can see how God operate acts 19:11 he prays for the dead and make alive the spirit in action. acts 19:11 he prays for the dead and make alive the spirit in action. When Paul was going to be arrest yes God save him from sin but the thing he done before he gets save, they charge him in the country he committed those crime, there were a man fill with the holy ghost's name Agabus tell Paul they are going to arrest you yes, they did but Jesus never leave him even in jail God say he is my prisoner that why we have to have good family, friends that when in good time and bad time they are with you the same like Jesus with Paul. Even in jail Paul pray and write one of his books he writes in the New Testament was from his jail cell to timothy and the church so it does matter where you are in the jail, home you have something positive to do go ahead and do it right now avoid negative people okay stay away from them giving you a head up, some people I have I get rid of them because they are wearing me do draining me out, they are demonic meaning satanic agent be careful and alert. I know a singer in jail and he still writing and singing song don't be limited by your situation God is an unlimited God big and powerful Jesus great awesome God faith arise in our soul only relationship can let you been efficient.

The spirit give you gift: for the God that we serve as my witness whom I serve with my spirit in the gospel we have to activate our gift that God gave us be not like the man in the bible that God gave him one gift and he hide it he never use it but the one that God gave 4 multiply it to 8, use the gift Jesus gave you like me Claudia, CeCe winna, Tasha cobb, Kim walker smith, kirk frankly, grace thriller, Hezekiah walker and our minister Jantzen franklin, john gray and other mighty man and women of God he see you. We have to know this very important the kingdom of God is not meat and drink but guess what it is? Righteousness, peace, joy and the holy ghost hope make not ashamed because the love of God is shed abroad in our heart by what the holy ghost, we must love with the holy ghost we cannot love in the flesh you will fail that why some much relationship break up because first to commence it was a fleshy relationship from beginning some of us was attracted to the shape, the color, the money that not love it flesh attraction. But Jesus love is unconditional is heart love, spirit love, selfless love when the money gone is love, when the flesh fail it still love get the thing in your spirit. The declaration from the great God says *for God so loves the world that he gave his only begotten son if you out there believe in his son Jesus serve him believe and serve him john 3 v 16. That this verse who me to serve Jesus because of the love he has for me and you out there, receive the true love Whitney Houston sing and I will always love you that supposed to be our anthem for love and not hate. Singer Denise brown say love and hate is not friend they are separate entities the people know us believer as children of God by his love in us and his spirit that the seal of approval the mark of Jesus family, do you have that seal from Jesus' answer. Watch Jesus love while we were yet sinner Christ die for us, taking this love greater, that what take him to the cross because of this great love not because we have something, we never have anything Jesus have everything to give us. So, Jesus gave us the ministry of reconciliation meaning is death on the cross reconcile us to God because the relationship was broken when the devil tempt eve to sin against God but the blood sacrifice Jesus shed bring the love back together, we are special people okay. So all my reader get Intune to heaven we need heaven news before the earthly news God bless us with all spiritual blessing in heavenly places in Christ Jesus look again how we are special people he chosen us before the foundation of the world that we should be holy and blameless, so let be blameless and holy the spirit give us wisdom and revelation in the knowledge of him just like when we go to school we try to learn as much, nothing wrong with that most important learn about the holy spirit and heaven operation that exceeding greatness of his power to all those who believe. Make sure we walk in humbleness and meekness apostle Moses was the meekness man on earth forbearing one another in God love and keep the unity of the holy spirit in the bond of peace you see the network of God kingdom. Very important information for all believer apostle Paul was preaching to the Ephesians church and those message is for us today he says "put on the whole armor of God meaning every day pray for it truth, the breast plate of righteousness, preach God word of peace, shield of faith, put on the helmet of salvation, the sword of the spirit which is the word of God praying always with all prayer and supplication in the spirit, pray for all these armor so we are properly cover that the devil flea. The gospel came not unto us in word only but it come with power and in the holy spirit through the sanctification believe in truth. This is warning to all believing all over the world just like we going to have disaster the weather man come and warn us before we have the storm, get the spiritual warning because we are living in the last days 1 timothy 4:1 and 2 the spirit speak expressly that in the last day some shall depart from the faith and giving in to doctrine of devil speaking lies in hypocrisy having their heart hardened, even what I personally see with the spiritual eyes some believer turn from God and taking the devil gift sell out God for money and fame that what timothy was saying I see it happening now so make sure you study the work and avoid the devil he is a deceiver and a liar is future is in hell so my friends chose Jesus in him we have a future bright and forth seeing. The holy spirit brings super natural miracle God bearing us witness both with sign and wonder and the gift of the holy ghost by the spirit Jesus make surety of a much better testament have an unchangeable priest hood. The holy spirit gives us faith in God that flesh cannot do faith coming by hearing and hearing by the word of God the patriarch obtain a better report because of their faith in God, the world was frame word spoken and the world come forth, Abel offers a better sacrifice that his brother Cain, by faith Enoch was translated that he should not see death because he please God are we pleasing God or man answer your question? By faith when Abraham was call by God to go to a different country he goes, by faith Abraham wife Sarah conceive and have a child at an old age we have to access God by faith and the spirit. We prophets have enquired and search diligently and prophesy of grace that should come to us by God. There is special preacher name pastor joseph prince have a ministry of grace that take over the world I personally like it, searching what manner of time the spirit of Christ which was in them. It reveals to us minister the thing that now reported unto us that has preach the gospel unto the holy spirit that send down from heaven to us all who are connected in Christ must have the holy spirit just like you can't drive a car until you have a driver license to drive, that the rule anywhere you go at lease on the public road. So, play by the rule and obey the ornament of a meek and quiet spirit which is in the sight of God of great price, humble ourself under the mighty hand of God so we will be exalted in due time casting all our cares on Jesus he cares for us.

Apostle john chosen of God: john was one of Jesus best disciple he was a lover and fill with the holy ghost that when Jesus was going to his father God, he says john take care of my mother he could ask the other disciple but he ask john. So, john say believe not every spirit but try the spirit whether they are of God, because many false prophets are gone into the world hereby know the spirit of God but the spirit that confess that Jesus Christ is come in the flesh is of God and the truth spirit give correct information read 1 john 4:1 to 3 make sure building yourself praying in the holy spirit and keep yourself in the love of God looking for the mercy of our lord Jesus unto eternal life have compassion making a difference. Jude 1:20 to 22. John was in the spirit when Jesus reveal the last day prophesy to him he was not in the flesh but Jesus say to john *I am the alpha and the omega the beginning and the end say the lord which is and which is to come the almighty what thou sees write in the book I gave you and send it to all the church, if we are hearing from God we should be producing good fruit like healthy life, great ministry, hit song, prosperity blessing and seeing thing in the spirit. I see Jesus in person when he calls me over 20 years, I hear his voice but never see him and I pray Jesus I need to see your face yes, I did see Jesus the risen king but he has a long veil over his face just like john the revelator it tell john the different message to give them read it all in revelation 2, 3. Every message he gave john he says here what the spirit says. All my reader see the important of the holy spirit it the cutting edge, the blue print to know who God is, it grow you in the fulness of our lord and savior Jesus Christ if you don't have the spirit pray spent time to get and maintain it keep it until Jesus come as Christian we cannot lose the spirit else we are spiritual dry we cannot afford that been Intune to the spirit world big time and Jesus, I am preacher on the holy spirit my finally verse on the holy spirit is apostle Paul writing 2 Corinthian 13:1 to 14 I write these things being present use sharpness according to the power which the lord gave me to edification and wisdom and understanding , finally all my reader be perfect, be of good comfort, be of one mind, live in peace and the love of God and peace shall always be with you, greet each other with the love of God, the grace of Jesus and the love of God and the communion of the special holy spirit be with you all amen. You can login every Sunday for me Claudia Henderson on live Facebook at 3pm USA time. Soon get a radio and television space we are working on it as I write this book, help me pray a day at a time: for prayer you can always come with us we are for you 754 368 9454 come with me to the next chapter we will be talking *prayer and love powerful blessing* amen and amen

CHAPTER 5:

GOD CREATED WITH LOVE

"For God so love the world he gave his only begotten son, if you believe in Jesus, you will not perish but have everlasting life" - John 3:16

God created this world in Love couple with the Holy Spirit from beginning we cannot trace the existent of God, but we believe he is a supernatural force that still existed, it a mystery God is spirit, so you have to have the spirit to really access God. The spirit is knowledge, wisdom and understanding and power with the secret of relation information about God that created all things on heaven and earth is all in our believe system. The process is the trinity God the Son Jesus and Holy Spirit different function but one God meaning just like the company Owner, Manager, Supervisor that how the kingdom operation but one God. So, the extension of God operation is more appointment he chosen to do is work are Apostles, Prophets, Bishops, pastors, minister, prayer warrior, angels that he sends daily to rescue us and prophets to foretell of what is going to happen. 2017 I was in New York when Jesus shows me in a dream the devastation of the world like tornado dream and now 2020 is lot of turmoil, you see when anything going to happen, he tells is prophets or apostle to warn before it happens that one that have a connection to God chosen people he calls, so people be careful of who preach and prophecy to you check if what they say happen.

The agape love of God the creator that gave the perfect gift to humankind his creation was in love with the Holy Spirit from beginning so if we are God children, we should have God love in our heart. In the beginning God created the garden in Eden he needs someone to dress and take care of it he created adman out of the dust to take care of it and then he finds out that Adam was lonely, so he put Adam to sleep and then take the rib out of Adam and made eve the women, so you see from beginning God is God of relation and love. Are we having the character of the Creator God peace, love, joy, giving and sharing I hope we are like God; Jesus is son when he was on earth demonstrate who our heavenly father was and is so if we are the extension of Jesus our genes must be the same character? God created man but he so sweet he gives us choiceless he not forcing us to love him are serve him we must chose to do I need the loving God are do I need the Devil that come to kill, steal and destroy you make a choice who you want to serve as 2020 and beyond.

I would recommend that every human being that living and breathing must serve Jesus God because he is sustain of quality life, good health, prosperity, he gives the gift of salvation God love is forever in good time and bad time. This world we are living everything about you the devil way is false and deceptive you don't want his way of doing thing you fell in love, and it don't take long for the relationship to break up because in the first place it was false love base on lies and false hope just pure flesh that not God love is fabricated. Check the statistic on married and how much end up divorce including believers it sad, because it wasn't love in the first place, I give the diamond, precious love of Jesus so rich and pure in good time and bad time is God unconditional love, whether you have money or not is God love, sickness and good health is money, whether the flesh fail is not God Love. I remember couple I was watching Trinity Broadcasting Network when I saw this couple, they were interviewing they were married but the wife goes out and have baby for a different man committed adultery, you would think the husband would divorce her no the husband was sad but after all he accepted her and welcome the baby in the family that not his and they love continue present that how much God Love us is people. When God Send his son Jesus his mission was to save us that was loss, broken, bad because God know we never know better we would need a loving savior Name Jesus call his :Jesus: meaning Salvation Names have biblical meaning so ask a believers that know what the meaning of your name., my name Claudia is in the bible as pilgrimage of the apostle Paul arm bearer the first human being created is Adam mean man Kind, Priest Aaron mean exalted one, father Abraham mean exalted father, Angel Gabriel mean God of my strength just give you few meaning of biblical names you can buy the book for biblical name "BREAKING THE JEWISH CODE" that a good book on Jewish laws and codes. Our real topic here is God Love.

The love of Jesus God Son extension of advance love that the people all over the world get until present Jesus let him do extra ordinary thing for God to get the glory Jesus would pray relentlessly for the perfect will of God to fulfill here on earth, he would demonstrate love in healing the sick, teaching in the temple, on street, in the mountain, in the home and he would feed the hungry take care of the poor, be where the reject or and the prostitute especially who society cast off. Jesus' mission is making sure people are accepted and welcome those who believe on him and even those who don't believe. Jesus say if we are calling on God and we are is children love is the first trait because love hang all the false prophets thou I preach, thou are pray do miracle and give millions of dollar and have not God love we are nothing you not reaching God at all., thou we speak with tongue of men and angels and have not love we are nothing, thou we prophecies and understand all mysteries and all knowledge and thou we have faith so we can remove mountain and have not love we are not God children, we identify our language as believers that have a relation with Jesus is real God Love not pretending and hate. Jesus' love bearish all thing cheating, poverty, hurt and pain but we still love despite the hurt peter betray Jesus, but Jesus forgives him and love him anyway Jesus says to Peter 3-time peter do you love me feed my sheep peter that us the people.

God blueprint, original love created love never fail until present 2020 everything fail but not the love of God I see some people think they would be in a job all there life but one day the boss decide to fire them, I see relationship break up after 50 year, 20 year, I see business that was created for 80 year but present in 2020 that business no more, I recall when the Police kill George Floyd here in America 2020 of March lot a store get rob I remember a jewel store in Miami was rob of all is diamond and gold the owner of the store say he will never recover and open what was loss. But Good new all my reader God, Jesus is love is always forever told he come that priceless gift cannot fail even when the storm blow it stand when hurricane come it still stand. 2019 I was Dallas Texas when I hear my phone beep off there is going to be a tornada but I really thought it was sick joke plenty of time my phone would beep when they looking for a car or somebody missing but this time the tornado really come and people loss their home and misplace for real., so make sure our foundation is solid love relationship, solid in Jesus that when the temper the devil come we can tell him no, when we are face with life challenges we are strong and well able like Caleb and Joshua. Now abide Faith which every believer should have, Hope that good but most highly important one is the unconditional, pure, agape love which the world cannot buy because it out of there reach. Read it all in 1 Corinthian 13 that best love chapter on Love by the Apostle Paul, it interesting Paul was a hater he would go all around the different temple in Israel and beat Christian, persecute then and even kill Christian that how hate Paul have but when Jesus Met Paul going to destroy the Christian he encounter Jesus and his whole life change completely., then we start have the unconditional love of God like some of us out there we use to hate each other, curse and carry news on each other but when we encounter the loving savior our life change completely pause a little and thank Jesus he change our life from hating each other to the full love of God is great change since Jesus come into our heart, mind and soul amen. The Greatest commandment is love with all our heart, mind and soul and love our neighbor as our self-God was talking sex because sex is not love so don't get confused reader Jesus' love is priceless, matchless, flawless it Just set by itself read exodus 20 for the commandment and do it not just read God word but do it let be in your heart day and night and mediate on them put it in practices. What the loving father God Hate and hate bitterly proud look, lying tongue, hands that shed innocent blood, heart that envy, war and devised wicked imagination, feet that swift to run in mischief, a false witness that speaks lies, and he that make decision in house of God my heavenly father hate evil big time from the beginning of the world God is holy and he defend holiness until present 2020 and beyond he will not compromise he say if your sin is like a mustard seed meaning these little lie, gossiping, idle talking if you are doing it stop because you shall not enter in God paradise and rest not just when you murder or rob but when you lie and cheat that how much Jesus value is love and he will not compromise it for nobody not even is chosen few Samson, Jazeel and Saul he love but they sin against God and he forsake them big time they never enter in God rest. The devil Satan was God right there next to God but Satan sin against God and rebel and God never spear him he was thrown out of paradise the bible say he come down with wrath in his mouth don't let the devil get a hold of you by let you hate, gossip, murder, steal, lie that how he get inside of you he need a body to use resist the devil and he will flee: Jesus also need of body, mind and soul God us body to preach, to pray, to fill with the Holy Spirit, to help other, so let Jesus be the house and headquarter where he can reside in every day all day. Just hear a new song recent in August of 2020 he goes like this {lord make me a house of prayer let the fire of my altar never burnt out} written by Eddie James I believe every Christian should sing this song prayer must become part of our lifestyle that how we communicate with Jesus on daily basis. And praise his only name we make up for the angels Satan take with him out of heaven.

The unusually love that people keep figuring out but anything Jesus created what you don't understand still accept what God do he know all things, there is priest in the bible by the name of Hosea he was virgin that never have a wife, but one fine day God says to Hosea there is prostitute in Israel by the name of Gomer because back in those days the children sin against God big time but the loving father need Israel know in spite of your sin I love you so much, so he send the man of God Hosea to bring them back to God. Some people would say God would never do that but if you believe in Jesus God and the Holy word name the Bible read in the Book of Hosea that proof of God love. God will send is people to love when nobody wants to love because of the person color, the person background, because of the person status and position that the kind of unusually love the master have for his people. See so many people do phony love but because I know how God operate it never surprise love is more powerful than money or fame love is a heart thing going down to the soul and mind, love must penetrate you whole being and blow your intelligent, Jesus love is not anything you can figure out, or program God business is unprogrammed only the Holy Spirit or Jesus can tell you what these thing mean no school cannot tell you, that why every Christian and believer must have the Holy Spirit because that how you will know God Secrets and understand in the supernatural realm of God. That mean you have to spend time in prayer and listening to what Jesus is saying quality time not just few minute or couple hour but some time days, week and month couple with year to know how his kingdom operate big time, some I am found guilty of time wasted but I start to alert myself and condition myself Girl in the presence of Jesus that where I really need to be to get the originally word, embrace, happiness and acceptance., all believe do the same if it even make time and drop thing that not necessary like lot of talking to friends and family for hour on the phone, sometime leave the television and social media for a while and access heaven. I remember when I start to have a real intimate relation with Jesus he would show me a lot film, lot heaven thing, recently January 2020 I was on a three (3) days prayer and fasting I remember clearly He bring me in a big pool and I was swimming and when I finally get out the Pool he take at a big Building huge place and there was lot camera on me and Jesus take me from the Crowd of people standing outside it was a lot of people and choose me and take me inside it was a lot of anointed angels singing praise to God that I experience I will never forget from the pool to hall of praising singer was amazing great to know Jesus God is real and operating in our life every day just believe., that why I tell people that to experience Jesus in relationship why is different from having a religion that cannot you with God, some place you go to worship is like a funeral service with people crying and boring and sad because Jesus is missing, the Holy Spirit is missing, no miracle, no prophesy, no anointed worship so of their worship is like funeral song and no love but hate and hostility, I see it for myself it sad to know.

Hope of God Love that keep us until he returns is what people need to have it not everybody going to marry here in this live but know you can still love by giving, going out with friends, make sure you always around loving people that can show you love in the form of embrace, little kiss on the jaw, laughing and joking around. I know a lot of people say to me I am not going to marry I will remain a virgin that what Jesus really need we remain seal until he come but he said in is word if you have trouble in the flesh get wife or husband and marry it better to marry than to burn, so you see from day one he never wants us to sex but to fellowship that is intention in the first place. When I was writing this manuscript, I see the oldest marry couple in the marry for 79 year and still going strong husband 110-year-old and wife 104-year-old that how it should be I know every relationship have their problems but real still stick together true good and bad time including this marry. God is mysterious in character in persona, in judgment and ways his ways are not like us and is thought is not like our though he is a reserve, merciful and meticulous God thank Jesus for those quality else a lot of us would not hear today, look how some people judgmental everything they quarrel, they condemn us but Jesus not like us he so much reserve and lay back he give you money we don't work for, he gave you position you are not qualify for, promotion you never earn Jesus give beauty for ashes., so dine, fellowship, connect with God so you will finally talk like him, act like him, behave like him and operate like him that when we spent quality time with our savior and high priest. God increase our physically, mentally, and spiritual life if we spent time in is present and believe him totally, God mercy extend to the non-believer that why we receive from him in spite of our unbelief but one day we have to change else he act like Sodom and Gomorrah that nation was sinning against God and he send prophets to warn them to stop else pending judgment will take place, Father Abraham negotiate with God save the people the prophets go back and preach to the stubborn people to repent they never heed until God destroy the people from the face of the earth. We are saying to everyone that reading this timely book is time to know Jesus as your personal Lord and Savior and stop wavering and Jesus love us and care about us deeply show back some love by give him your heart mind and soul that proving to the heavenly father God, you truly love him., love is doing not just talking but action speak louder than word. Let God transpiring love reach in your soul and heart be careful where love come from When Abraham need a wife for his son Isaac he was very careful where that wife come from where Abraham live those people worship false God and he never want is son to stray from the living God so he send his arm bearer to the land where make they connect in the Holy Spirit, they believe in the truth God they love like the way you love Them not one sided love and action must be in that love., next thing pray to God if is the right person for you before you say your " I DO " that a serious vow we are making so being sure else you will to regret that you do. Love is the best gift any human being must have in their heart it the greatest gift God gave to humankind us it kindly, gently, freely. Solomon was a next lover that know how to love in the first half of his life, but God tell him there are certain women you don't talk because they will turn their heart from you bad influence and peer pressure can cause great pain and loss, so Solomon disobey God and enter into a relationship with these jezebel women and loss the throne is father David left him with that great loss one time can cause you a life time.

Love that go the extra mile that money cannot go when the money done true still continue forever make sure you have true love bake in your heart, I hear about over a year this women right here in the USA won millions of dollar in lotto he promise is Pastor some of the money to extent the building of the temple when the time come for the women to give over the money she change her mind and tell the man I cannot give the money again because I have to help my expected husband that was disappointed. The point I am trying to make priority has lot to do with us she loves her expected husband that much that she was will to turn down the man of God which I disagree, she should have split the money because God work is most important than a family because when we put Jesus first then everything come after meaning pray first thing in the morning, worship and read God word and then giving your tithe and offering whether small or big because buy doing that you see advance increase. This rich ruler in the bible when he approaches Jesus to talk, she gives all your position to the poor the man tells Jesus no I can do that so there he preferred money over Jesus that it with some of us money, fame, family is our idols that why we lose out on Jesus and his love, blessing and peace so next time you making simple decision or major decision bottom line put Jesus first. So, getting a job you have to work on Sunday or Saturday that the main time you worship what you going to you tell Jesus what is your finally answer? I would tell the employee sir or madam I can work on that particular day because I have to attend the house of God, he is worth all of our time and sacrifice. Relationship with Jesus is highly important it play out in your everyday life and put you in a safe zone all the time we see life for what it all about and not what it not about. Just like you marry to your husband you know than anybody else because you are with him every day that how relationship with Jesus every day you know everything about because you spent time with Jesus is our everyday friend Abraham become a friend of God because he obey God command and dear to be different., Love make Abraham bring is only son Isaac to be slaughter when God say bring you son to alter but he obey and when the time come to salute God immediately send scape goat that prove to God Abraham really and truly love Jesus and become the father of us all because of obedient amen. He says blessed of them that leave family, job, friends for my sake I Jesus will repay you will never regret it, you walk away from a life of fame and prestige, but Jesus will repay. This singer in Jamaica her name Minister Marian Hall was at the height of her career making lot of money, travelling the world when Jesus call say come follow me my sister right now she is singing for Jesus and making more music and still touring the world, she could easily say Jesus I am not leaving my career because everything was perfect thank God she did thank you my sister people need to hear these glorious testimony so they can think of serving the true and living that give us song to sing, instrument to play music, Holy Spirit word to preach and touch life all over the world to God be the Glory. The next love story this pastor was lock up in prison for crime in did but when he was in solitary confinement here come Jesus to him I have been calling so long and now is the time you give me your heart, mind and soul, he said when he look in the jail it was a bible and he start reading the bible because confinement read you are alone 23 hour a day you are not in the population of the prison., Jesus release him from the prison right now he is all over the world sharing the good news of Jesus is peace love and joy, some of us get heal, deliver, provide for and save rescue from sin that the working love of God uncensored spent time and praise and thank him for all he done and he is going to do right now. He may not come when you want but he will surely be until like Lazarus was bury in the tomb for 4 day when Jesus suddenly arrive on the seen the family was upset with Jesus late coming, but Jesus prove again to us is not time and space it right time matter of course Jesus pray faith prayer and the dead man come alive, this mother have is son in the coffin and Jesus see the morning crying for his only begotten and Jesus just touch the coffin one time the dead childlike Lazarus was immediately raise from the dead, God timing not man timing., get this in your spirit and rest assure. You may not get the opportunity to go to school but Jesus is home schooling you right now in 2020 so many school are close because of corona virus but at home Jesus is teaching you when I was typing this book in September 2020 I get a call from my family my 16 year old niece say I am home school I simple tell take up your book at home read and ask my daughter to help you, I am saying to you do the same parents or guardian help the children with their school work until school return.

So children in Africa, Haiti, Indian, America and some country their children never get the opportunity to sit into a class room and yet some of them still learn at home and are living Great live, some never get the opportunity to have food, house and basis thing we take for guarantee but yet God help them big time., Jesus will help you too be hopeful, believe your dream will come true soon., be positive, be optimistic and keep expected it will happen stay with Jesus never let him go he is the one that can help you. 2019 When I start this book I write and put down the manuscript was searching for publisher so many of them call me about the book because the title they like at least some of them, But now 2020 of all the publisher is just one keep calling me for the book to publish partly every day there on then I know is the Lord working true this young Lady to come to me that how Jesus use people to help in a diplomatic way I was challenge to finish this book because God know lot of people will be bless and encourage in this challenging time., make sure you have people like this young lady to encourage to next level of your life, people with passion, Zeal, with motivation with good intention and have your interest at heart Jesus will make your connection for you just let him, let go and let God, get out of Jesus way so he can do is work in us true us. When negative people come in your life the devil send them tell them clearly go back where you come from don't let them settle down in your life you will live to regret every moment of it don't entertain angel on aware. In April of 2020 in the height of the pandemic I take in a young lady I don't know of the street until present I sorry I did she was negative and demonic. So be always on the alert ask Jesus for Spirit of discernment you see thing before it happens that demon take me unaware thank Jesus, I was safe it best you say no or yes before danger come.

Apostle John was the greatest lover of the 12 apostle nobody can love like John that When Jesus was leaving to go to his father out of 11, he says John take care of my mother because Jesus know that john love was special than any other apostles, prophets love is gift the world need in this hateful world. I see people hate for nothing, want to hurt you for nothing, want to destroy you for nothing hate you for nothing despite the negative vibe, our job is to show God Love by talking kind word, by sharing, by volunteering and witnessing to the lost. Love is God light on the earth is what defeat the devil not fighting or cursing but Love that never die. Picture Jesus when he was arrested, he never resists arrest he go willingly, when the enemies put him in jail, he is willing to go, love get advance when they strip of his rope they beat him, piece is side blood come bash him aggressively Jesus never fight back, because love tell him know. Do we have that love in our heart? Are we faking love for things make sure he has that pure everlasting love that lost forever? God is love and he created the world in love and relationship.

Code from the apostle John the greatest lover of the 12 apostles: "I rejoice greatly that I found of the children walking in truth as we have received a commandment from the father, and now I beseech thee lady not as though I wrote a new commandment unto thee, but that which we had from the beginning that we "LOVE" the golden word one another and this is love that we walk after God commandment that as ye have heard from the beginning we should walk in it.

Final on the chapter about GOD and LOVE having many things to write unto you, I would not write with paper and ink: But I trust to come unto you all face to face that our joy may be full, blessing. Read the book of Solomon, John the Book of the bible of a lot of Love about God and Jesus. Come with me to the next chapter about RESTORATION

CHAPTER 6:

RESTORATION AND VICTORY

"Jesus will restore to you all the years that the locust had eaten the cankerworm Abd the caterpillar and palmerworm my great army which I send among you, and we shall eat in plenty say Jesus and be satisfy and praise the name of the lord our god my people shall never be ashamed the enemies shall know God is still with us." - Joel 2:25 to 27.

We know that is the last days we are living so much bad thing is going when I go out to do mission so many people complain say preacher if there is real savior or God why my wife, children, my coworker my neighbor die, why I am homeless, why I am rejected, why I am broke, why nobody like me and I could go on and on about the why's. But my answer is there is still a Savior that love us and care despite what is happening, Jesus the master goes true a lot for us to present here so we people will go true a period of suffering too but the good news it not going be for long. Just be positive about the situation we are in now keep believing that Jesus will come true for us and don't give up don't cometh suicide are thrown in the towel. Your empty bank account will be fill, your body will be heal, your missing family will come home including husband, wife children and extending family, have faith in God faith mean you don't see an ending in the physical situation, but keep believing, keep hoping and put action to you faith for example you need a job go fill out the application, go look and ask around after you pray, you need a husband or wife go social to party, house of God, fellowship in mall just causal walking be a friendly person not selfish, that working faith with prayer and believing will equal success and achieving what you need from Jesus., We talking RESTORATION.

Stop looking at the situation you are facing and start looking at the big God we serve just like King David he wasn't looking at the big giant Goliath is focus was the big God that fill Him with the Holy Spirit on fire and of course David won the giant big time. So, people don't be intimidated by people face, or height, or aggressiveness now that when you enter into a relationship covenant with Jesus and you are obedient to Jesus you win in finances, you win in relationship, you win in good health you win in God because your heart is in Jesus, your mind and soul is rap up and tangle up in Jesus and that how he need us to be every day all day and not just some time or when we feel like. We are the temple the body is where Jesus lives so we have made sure it Holy, pure and clean with Jesus' love, peace and joy. Restoration of the first with children of Israel when the was in Egypt in slavery for thousands of years their task master Pharoah and his helper work them to death and beat them, pay them little and nothing just like some of you out there can relate to this store owner or boss work you out for long hours and pay you little wages that how they treat these people in Egypt. But fine day God Send Moses and Aaron to Egypt to free from the great transgression of human bondage. So, Moses and Aaron go and finally liberate them free at last say Martin Luther King

Nelson Mandela was one of the now a days slave they hold him captive for so much year in jail in South Africa but he never give up Hope one fine day Jesus with our prayer release him from cruel hands of the transgressor., Joseph was one of them that was lie upon by his own family when the God of Isaac, Jacob, David the God of Claudia and many more believe call you name free from the cruel hand., so much restoration story from the pastor, prophets, members, bishop from just ordinary people of the goodness of Jesus. This 2020 I saw a news where this wife and husband was in car accident when they go to hospital the doctors pronounce them dead, they say in the coma Jesus came in the room and say you are alive and he touch both of them and they came back to live with every broken bones heal all loss was the car which can be replace., so many people get heal recently from corona virus this couple right here in US was recently heal from cancer and them they battle corona virus and Jesus miraculously heal husband and wife. The woman with the issue of blood in bible have blo0d condition for over 12 year she goes to all the doctor and lot place no one could help her, but when Jesus came on the scene she reaches out to Jesus and her believing faith make her whole it was million at that healing service but her whole focus was to get her healing because she was hurting so bad, I hear a man say when I am in trouble anything to get me out I will go for it. King Saul was one of the desperate man in deep trouble with the Lord because he was very disobedient King he let his position God gave him turn a curse on him Jesus lock off speaking to him period that where his blessing come from and it was taken away, so Saul was seeking other channel for help so he go to witches in Israel to help him out of desperation, but he get a surprise of his life instead of help the witches tell tomorrow this time you going to die that the last thing nobody want to hear., yes that particular witch was right the other day Saul went into battle with enemies and die with his son. Somebody reading this book would say why God never restore him simple because Saul was taking order from God anymore, he was rude and pride take him over, don't let pride take you over and disobedient that the root cause of evil and disgrace. Is not every problem will be restored because Jesus knows us all he knows our heart and intentions, some situation is just mercy and grace help us not to be destroy but when we continue in sin and not stopping then we are in big trouble with Jesus, so stop doing wrong and make it right with God now 2020 and beyond?

When I was living in Jamaica this story will make you realize that when we can stop doing wrong thing we end up in trouble this women marry over 8 different husband and 7 of the husband die under his care because the women was wicked his alias name was "the white witch of rose hall" now the last husband he marry kill this wicked woman you see is because she never have no intention of stop murdering., that what with some of us especially some believers we say we are believers but when we leave the house of God we gossip, lie, sex out of married, cheat on her husband and wife, early this year 2020 about march I see this story of this pastor just let his flesh take a hole of him so start seeing some of the church sister and go in the pulpit and preach like he never do nothing wrong right now he is living with AIDE disease it a result of us not stopping sin, I also sure Jesus try to tell stop and get married to one but he was not listening to Jesus voice. If this pastor is reading this book or those who are sinning against Jesus is full time you stop go down on your knee and say Jesus forgive me of my sins and trans passes create in me a clean heart oh God a renew a rite spirit in me. Restoration means taking responsibility for what you do wrong and blaming other people for your mistake because you need to experience Jesus' restoration and acceptance and love in your spirit. I know you read the bible and see so much restoration stories and you read newspaper and watch television and social media see other stories of God Goodness I know you need it in your personal life too if can have it if you believe and change your heart and life

The apostle David is stories of victory and pain he was man after God own heart he won many battle for Jesus but one fine day David see a young lady having Shower naked outside, he could not let his lusting go away he send for the young lad Bathsheba and sleep with the man wife, Bathsheba was a marry women but David could help himself he slept with her and then have her husband kill in the battle yes reader King David a man after God own heart, God prize possession but David sought the Lord for forgiveness fervently with an open heart of be sorry for his sins and crime he committed and God forgive let me take you to David confession: " have mercy on me oh God according to thy loving kindness according unto the multitude of they mercies blot out my transgression, wash me thoroughly from mine iniquity and cleanse me from my sin are we out there surrender to Jesus for the sin we committed in our life at present. David, say I acknowledge my transgression and my sin is ever before me, against thee only have I sin and done this evil in thy sight that thou lightest be justify when thou speak and be clear when thou judge, create in me a clean heart and renew I right Spirit within me read it in is entirely Psalm 51 all for it. So, it does not matter what sin we have committed we can go down on her knee with sincere heart like take and ask Jesus to forgive us he will because he sees in the heart, David was restored after such a horrific crime committed, so even if you murder you can ask Jesus to forgive us, or steal, or committed fornication or adultery the only sin that Jesus don't forgive us when we sin against the Holy Ghost that the only sin will not forgive. So don't let believers or non-believer condemn you when you sin all there is you go down on you knee before the loving father and he will forgive us, you don't have to run away stay and deal with it like real man or women. This is restoration of forgiveness this woman married, and she was cheating on her husband and have baby for the other man that not her husband you would think the husband would break up the relationship he forgives his wife and adopt the baby and continue with their relationship Oh yes that Jesus unconditional love of victory and restoration. The woman on April 22, 2019 was with cancer and Jesus heal her I see some much business close down because of the virus and different reason but I can tell you some many people boasting success of Jobs, some win money, some business are still operating and good business going on, even so much people are still getting married including me because is a mindset we are in this world but we are not a part of what happening in this world, it don't affect us like who are caught up with what happening so be careful of what hit your mind and focus.

Restoration of the last like that woman at ziarat that have the last oil left she was down to nothing and they were coming to take her son and everything she own but the prophet Elisha was just in time to rescue her from this great shame, he told her get all the pot and fill it with Oil and she did and from the last to have millions of dollars because she was obedient to what the prophet tells her to do. The reason some of us don't restore because we are disobedient and want to do thing our way it does not work like that in the kingdom of God, it work by what Jesus need us to do, that why we have some much religion and few believer connected to God because we doing her way and right now lot temple are closing down because it was not of God, The bible say and these word are prophetic {upon this rock I build my church and gate of hell will not prevail} we can add on to God word he tell Moses tell the children of Israel don't add to my word else I will add the plaque they see in Egypt that how serious God is with his word and commandment and covenant. Make sure as believer we keep them are stand the consequences just like there is law we have to abide by anywhere in the world you live 2018 when I was in London they have many law when I go to the queen palace at Buckingham place you can't go inside unless you have invitation, there are certain limit to go because police all over to enforce the law, right here in the USA you can drink beer outside, we have to drive certain speed limited else we get ticket or warning, we have stay certain limited from white in Washington again police are there 24 hour day to enforce certain law and of course protect the president, In Jamaica island if you steal, murder you gone to jail, even in your home mother and father have room for the children certain time to go to bed, manners and respect is must, like when we were growing up as Children our parents tell us have manner and respect to each other is same in God kingdom we all must mandatory to obey by God rule and regulation or hell is our doom and torment, nobody want to suffering don't you answer your question do you want to suffer? I don't think so everyone needs a good life of love acceptance, property, peace, having good husband and wife and enjoy Jesus' salvation and good health especially in this time 2019 and 2020 when so much virus going around, we need Jesus Blood covering and shelter around us and family. In 2020 I was praying early morning and when I finish the prayer, I sat at driver seat waiting for Jesus to reply back Jesus come in person with a big umbrella and say to me daughter you are well cover that particular day I feel like somebody give me a billion of dollar because the creator the savior makes me feel special and protected and reassure all my reader you are very much protected by Jesus. Some these famous people with money have bodyguard following them but only Jesus and his Blood can cover us under is precious blood do you believe in what we saying it truth because Jesus want me to share these timely messages true book, word of mouth social media and all other channel including bus, train, plane and house of God. This restoration story this 20 year old man have the last $2us in his pocket and he say he was going to buy beer but when he went unto the store he hear a voice buy the lotto and he from was trying to ignore the voice but finally he buy the lotto right here in America and yes he won millions of dollar of wicket rom only $2 with empty bank account only dead job he say when he get pay and pay bills nothing left like all of your story out there right now he is with elite of this world they report say he richest than some famous star. Now you would say Christian not to gamble but Jesus says the wealth lay on the just you do your research who is the wicked before you start make judgement read the bible and know these things in the word of God.

Just like I was examine some of these no tradition song by Michael Jackson, Whitney Houston, Luther Vandross, Bob Marley and Denis Brown I Jesus was with when I start listen to word of the song and I arrive that the lyrics was clean and could be dance to sing, so guess what I have a Live Facebook Show every Sunday at 3p,m, USA time I start play them for the people and let them know they can listen to because it just love peace and Joy I would challenge every believe listen to these artist and play them instead of been legalistic about these timely song. Restoration is what you allow yourself to listen, read and do and this is powerful, because the truth is some of these songs, message can make you are break you it between you and Almighty God. Restoration of the most notorious man in the bible from an abuser and murder to God chosen vessel just like Ital the wicked man that kill off the Jews that how wicked Saul was he would persecute Christian, pull out the temple and home and persecute them he was a part of how Stephen was stone to dead and Paul was false Christian just like some of us pretend to be what we are not. But when Paul encounter Jesus is whole life of shame become one of restoration and glory to God, he was down for 3 days and 3 nigh before he was completely change and write most of the New Testament so believe you going to stop gossip, lie, cheat, falsify God in 2020 and beyond Jesus will transform your life and your enemies will be ashamed do you want your life to change? Are you satisfying with how you are live? We all need to search her heart before we start blaming people or casting stone and when we do that and change to transforming power of Jesus Christ, we start see victory every day. Ruth of to leave his pageant nation that never believe in God to be restore, Abraham too have to leave his pageant nation to be father of us all so do some shifting meaning if you have to leave some friends, leave a job, leave where you worship even leave family because when look back and see they are negative talker, they don't believe in your God, they never have anything good contribute to your whole be it time to walk away and say bye you are no more welcome here., there is song by Jonathan Nelson say you no more welcome here it so true I play that song in my time of worship to God even if is your pastor, bishops or member it sometime painful we don't want to hurt people but you have to do and please Jesus and pray to Jesus for clear direction including where should I worship, where to live, who should I have for friends Jesus wish job should I have only he have the perfect answer. I learn over the year when I do something out of God will I fail badly and end up broken and injure so like me Claudia pray to master for direction don't we all need victorious life well pleasing to God and us, the bible say as for me and my house I will serve the lord come what may it so nice when every family member can pray together at home, live in harmony, live in peace and love that the world cannot give only Jesus can give stability and real life try it on your own and see how it goes if you don't believe Jesus restoration life and know you will fail and fail badly, so my personal challenge as author of this timely book do it Jesus way and it will save you time and resources.

So many prophets in the bible stray from the will of God and loss out on God big time at the end never see true victory because the turn from God ways and do it there ways Moses was the one that liberate the children of Israel and guess what Moses end up never see the promise land because of what he said to the Israelite, God say I show the promise land but you can go into it that sad, why because even then the people was bad and ungrateful God never please with word Moses talk in the end, just like you have a bad child and somebody say something bad about your own kid as parent you not going to feel good about the insult on your child even dough you know your child is bad, we is the same thing with Moses the beginning was great but the was disastrous only Caleb and Joshua see the promise land flowing with milk and water. So realistic we got to be careful the word from her mouth. Here in the USA the least thing people sue us and even want to hurt because simple words some people end up in jail because of word that spoken to them the bible call it filthy communication no gossip word I sat and hear sometime people talk and I was surprise of the nasty word spoken, even sometime some preacher preach filthy communication that not of Jesus simple they can't preach back to me because God Jesus correct in love, not warily word, or word of destruction those thing is not of

God is the devil character. So, every born-again believer must have the Holy Spirit in their heart and soul to know right from wrong that the light that must turn on at all time it alerts us of what is going on right or wrong.

When Joseph was in the pit and prison that was is finally destination even in those adverse condition the dream he had before all these bad thing happen to him in his heart they were still alive he know at the end he would be the greatest leader of all time like Michael Jackson from a poor background to the greatest singer ever live, Whitney Houston from peasant girl singing in choir at church to be the greatest singer every live until today 2020, Elvis Presley from poor background to greatest singer ever life, serena William from a poor family, be rejection because of her color and background to the best tennis player in the world, Tyler Perry from Homeless man to the best actor in the world latest Forbes magazine have in 2020 as newest billionaire, Oprah Winfrey from a poor girl be abuse by family to be the world richest billionaire., Jeff Bezos from be adopted to own amazon, American internet entrepreneur, industrialist, investor right now present 2020 the richest man in the world. These famous people was just regularly people like me and you but they have big dream and work toward them and achieve them so you can do it, Jesus our messiah was born in lowest of the lowest in stable where horses should be but that never stop our high priest from becoming who God our holy make him to be the healer, the Savior, the King man redeemer lover of her soul, the Jehovah shalom the great of the greatest walk this earth he walk on water and never drown Jesus deviled gravity and win even in his last day on plenty earth. So every have purpose start fulfill your purpose before it too late what your heart telling, what Jesus telling you right now reading this manuscript put down the book a little and start ask Jesus what shall I do and he will answer if you are at noisy location go to quiet location because this is your life we talking about and we only can live one life on earth that was given by creator God especially were still living in this 2020 century we something solid that can last until Jesus come back for a ready people. Gift and talent were meant to use not sit on activate you God given gift and start use it immediately even reading the book start if singing, working, healing, helping do something with its Whitney Houston never condition herself she just going to sing in Church no she uses her gift all over the world and in the end famous like King Jesus our Lord and King. Restoration must start with us and where our life going for the future don't let the devil limit you with background or status jump over his head and fulfill what Jesus have you to do or let the devil advocate stop your destiny there is singer in Jamaica name Budju Banton singing timely song name destiny You can listen that song it very uplifted and encourage the prophet Habakkuk say write your vision and make it plain in book that you may run with it and do it for the vision is yet for an appointed time but at the end it shall speak and not lie, though it tarry wait for it to materialize and see it profit. Habakkuk 2:2 to 4 read this scripture I am giving you and meditate on it day and night until it happens.

Restoration of world leader and icon it amazing how Jesus work in amazing way Prophet Daniel was taken in exile and some of the Israel Jews because they sin against God but even in exile God chose Daniel to be his end time prophet, so The King Nebuchadnezzar favor Daniel and love and ask Daniel to interrupt his dream because is astrology could not do it shame when you own worker cannot to the work they supposed to do my God, so King Nebuchadnezzar to Daniel in exile of a truth if it is that your God is a God of God and a Lord of king and a revealer of secrets let him reveal this secret for me, and Daniel reveal all the king secrets and promote Daniel to be great in Babylon from exile to ruler over the whole province and chief of the government over all the wise men of Babylon., and the exile get promoted was Shadrack, Meshach and Abednego over the affairs of the province of Babylon but Daniel sat with the king. Can you imagine from be in jail to release and get promoted that real big victory from God? Now when President Obama was running for the election here in America most people believe he never have a chance but I also sure Obama believe in himself he could have won he were looking at the odd because the odd was against but God Jesus make him prove all the odd were wrong and the next obstacle most American though it was just one term but thank Jesus it was the full 2 term it important when you believe in Jesus and believe in yourself before anyone believe in you, we got like ourself as how God created us we may be different in language, or culture or way of doing things but the end must be I can do all thing true Christ wish give me strength that the Apostle Paul code you sure can be the best wife, best husband, the best cleaner, the best worker, the best policemen or women, the best doctor, lawyer, nurse, business man or women, the best million or billionaire, the best bus driver anything you do make it be the best of our ability. Be the best man and women of God it does matter the gift God gave you do with everything in you, when Jesus say come from the work place and start preach on the buses in Jamaica I never for one day say I am not doing it because it to low nothing is low when Jesus tell you to do, so clean the church, some open the door, some visit those who are in the prison and jail do it, so preach and prophesy use what God gave you without complain and care what negative people say, stay with positive people of God that can see you restore to where Jesus need you to be. The prophet Samuel when he was young little boy he have Eli as his mentor Eli was priest in Israel so his mother never make a mistake to leave his baby Samuel in good hand, The apostle Paul mentor Titus and timothy in ministry and both son end up to be the preacher of your time because it was Godly connection, some make sure you have Jesus connecting you to the right spiritual mother and father in body of Christ these people are like you biologically parent they make you are break the end product must resulting in Holy life, Spirit Fill, obedient and producing Godly fruit from those year of mentoring good fruit. Those disciples were mentorship by Jesus himself but one Judas get the word at the end stray from Jesus word and betray him is not because Judas never get the word why he done that evil but because he was pay to do and the bible say the devil enter judas so people out there keep your heart unto Jesus fill with God word every day, have the Spirit in you, resist the devil and he will go I like the song Tasha Cobb sing say: " fill me lord till I overflow I want to be like you and overflowing every day and it start with quality prayer, fasting, praise and reading the holy bible" so the devil will be less until he is afraid of you because your persona is God, the word from your mouth is positive so he is an unwelcome guess that how you get rid of demon and devil and of course say the BLOOD OF JESUS you will be retore and victorious,

When you are radical and every day having on the whole armor you are dangerous to the devil wherefore take unto you the whole armor of God that we may be able to withstand in the evil day having all our armor stand, having your loin gird about with truth so speak truth, having the breastplate of righteousness, our feet shod with the preparation of gospel of peace, above take the shield of faith wherein we may be able to quench all fiery darts of the wicked all believer must have these shield, take the covering the helmet of salvation and the sword of the Spirit which the word of God every believer must have the true Spirit of God to lead us and teach us, praying always with prayer and supplications in the spirit and watching in the Spirit with all perseverance and supplication for all the saints. So, after we get the different armor in our church which is the body utterance will be given unto us so we may speak God word boldly to make know the mystery of the glorious gospel to all nation around the world. Ephesian 6:12 to 24. We as Christian we wrestle not against flesh and blood, but against principalities, against power, against the ruler of the darkness of this present world 2020 and beyond and against spiritual wickedness in high places. So we have to wear God armor every day all day and be alert like the Police, soldier and security personnel when you see them on duty they always prepare with their gun, and everything needed to fight enemies so we as born again Christian and children of the most high God must prepare and ready every day with word of God, our praise and the word in our heart because it a battle every day we are no more serving the devil we are on Jesus side so he use people to come against meaning to curse us, steal from us, to destroy us but we can attach in back by saying devil we plea the blood of Jesus her with against you, have victory word God is great he fight her battle every day just stand and see Jesus fight for us all we do in return praise him and give glory to his name. I leave the chapter of Restoration with song that when the children of Israel leave the bondage in Egypt prophetess Miriam sing this victorious song: "took a timbrel in her hand and all the women went out after with timbrels and with dances and prophetess Miriam lead the victorious Israelite in victory praise for, he hath triumphed gloriously the horse and his rider hath thrown into the sea. The Lord is my strength and song, and he is become our salvation he is our Great God that defend his people until present we will prepare his habitation our father God, we all will exalt Jesus for taking us out of the devil courtyard," read this victory song Exodus 15 all of it. I know some of my reader can shout of the goodness of Jesus you were heal, deliver, provide for when there was no way out, Jesus pay off your house, all your bill were pay when it look impossible, when the doctor tell I can treat your sickness no more Doctor step over ordinary and get into the supernatural and heal the cancer, the corona virus, the lupus, the anxiety and stress and most important save your precious soul from going down to hell open mouth and say thank Jesus spent some time and talk Jesus in prayer and praise unto the most high God. I pray for more victory every day amen.

CHAPTER 7:

HOLY SPIRIT AND THANK GIVING TO JESUS

"When Jesus receives the Holy Spirit, he went straight into the wilderness and pray and fast forty day and forty nigh to gain power and authority." - Matthew 4:1 and 2

So we the role the Holy Spirit play in our life every day if we are followers of Christ we must have the special Holy Spirit last year 2019 I was doing mission work for Jesus in Texas state when Jesus say start study more on the Holy Spirit and did for sure because every believer need the Godly gift the Holy Spirit mean for who don't know it teach you the deep thing of God, it give the super natural power, and give God wisdom, knowledge and understanding it only Jesus can give this gift no bible school or seminary can give it to you but Jesus. Looking on the Holy Spirit from beginning when God start created this present world and the earth was without form and void and darkness was upon the face of the deep and the Spirit of God move upon the face of the water Genesis 1:2 that telling me the important of this special gift where you worship to the pastor believe in the Holy Spirit because if they do not believe show them in the bible that no believer can serve Jesus God without it is must we have the Holy Spirit. As you read this book as believer and you don't have the Holy Spirit start praying to get it anywhere you are at Home, your temple, your work place it does matter you location you need to have to function in prophetic realm of Jesus Christ or any level you are in Christ It does matter how long you are save if still can receive it if need it, we know you have to need something to get, just like our body need water, food, exercise to function is same with the Holy Spirit the manifestation of the Spirit is great reward in our personal life you see spiritual growth of more seeing Jesus, hearing the secret of Jesus telling it to you, when you pray in the Holy Spirit you see great result prayer answer, but make sure when the Holy Spirit tell you something do it or you never see result obedient go hand in hand with Holy Spirit source and of course with Jesus with us always. We Thank Jesus for is perfect gift to us to equip us to do good work for his glory to be achieve here on earth. Noah was preacher of righteousness and he preach the repentance messages for some many year because God gave him and all his chosen people this special gift of the Holy Spirit so we are not on our own, Father Abraham was God main man that he raise up from nation of the Haram those people never believe in God but Abraham and his family believe in God and God spoke Abraham in dream say leave that county and let you know where I need you to go a mean Abraham was over 75 year old he and his wife Sarah they could easily say I am not going because I make my life in my country but God fill him with Holy Spirit and the whole family obey God and left that forbidden land. Hear God word to Abraham {Get thee out of thy country and from the kindred and from thy father house, unto a land that I will shew and High God will make thee a great nation powerful word from the creator God when the last time you hear Jesus speak to you? Are we listening when Jesus speak are we do busy when he talk and listening, and I will bless thee and make you and your family a great nations and you Abraham shall be a blessing of my favor upon you God goes on to blow Abraham mind of more blessing from God and in your father Abraham all families of this earth will be bless because you obey the Almighty God} and exactly what God told Abraham he do and inherited God unmerited favor read all in Genesis 12:1 to 5.

When do faith, obedient and have the Holy Spirit and do what his told to do then we finally enter into unbroken able covenant with the creator of the university and even your enemies will be at peace with you., we learn to ignore demonic people, learn to obey Jesus even if people reject you, the boss fire, even if your life uncomfortable Jesus will set you up more and greater blessing than what people give. 2020 and beyond you are not ordinary your just any and anybody you are

God prize possession black or white, rich or poor when Jesus is your inspirator and motivator you can rest assure you are safe in his arm. Take a good look at Abraham story it take a lot God in his heart to do what God tell consider he was from a different county where those people never worship or serve God just like some Islamic region, some quaker religion that where Abraham coming from but great news he make a choice to hang to God that to me looking like big gambling going to the casino and lotto to spent money and gambling you don't know if you going to win but you say come what may I trying my luck with all my pay cheque I get., You can win or lose. That how Father Abraham makes a choice and choose Jesus he was more bless than what he has in Haram the Godless nation. I move by Abraham story it give more faith in God knowing that apart of such a great heavenly host my daddy is Jesus God when Jesus was leaving earth he was finish with us yet, he say to the 11 apostles I send you a comforter his name his the HOLY SPIRIT that the caring savior his name is JESUS serve him out there, in this modern world we are living some people are so selfish and aggressive sometime I cry like baby we are reaching out to them and some of these people are insulting us I have been there done that. Because I am missionary, I have to interact with different people from different country and different background and culture, so time just talking to them about Jesus is insult and some day when you go bang on their door to witness and share the word of God to them is insult and door slam in our face missionary and evangelist would surely know what I am talking about. But some good news some of the people are very nice some really leaving the home and come tell them about Jesus I remember I lady say thanks for coming my dear she was 1 out of hundred that welcome us she hosts me in return with all good things bless the Lord. So, all my reading we really need a heavy spirit of friendly just like we have the Holy Spirit we to be out right friendly meaning don't wait for people strike up conversation you can first start one with them be smiley, be jovial, be entertaining and not boring so they want to hear what you have to say. Different way to present the Love gospel without being boring and legalistic my God if they don't want to hear just be nice in love and say goodbye without ill feeling. His like you have a business, and some customer is rude and boisterous you not going to curse them out even there are bad just ask them kindly to leave or ignore period if they draw weapon will call the Police but the last thing you want to do is curse them out. Because some boss would fire you whether wrong or write before you get the job some boss or supervisor would detail what to do and how to treat different personality customers and I almost sure that the main thing they would tell the worker to argue with customer it does matter how bad they are, if happen to go to school or college and trade school they will lecture you about personality trait or how to communicate with customer or client. When I was going to college and trade school, they would tell us that don't argue with my clients or customer I clearly remember and it so true. Doing the missionary service, I try to apply the same rule not all the time I am perfect, but I try to hold my tongue between my teeth I tell my friends that we preacher, missionary and evangelist get more attack than any other worker out there, but when Jesus calls us praying every day and asking his help and protection making very easy for us preacher and some preacher would agree.

You have to have 1 day out of every week to fast and pray without eating but of course you pray every single day even if you are regularly member living the right way for Jesus you will still come under attack especially when you real from Jesus but as say don't answer back and praise Jesus and plea the blood of Jesus that the weapon against the enemies. We believers need to stay health and connected to Jesus and the spirit we have to have spiritual food every single day and spent quality time with God, I show the various apostles that was successful having the powerful Holy Spirit and they please God glory take Jacob that stole is brother birthright but God was looking at his action he was looking deeper than that so many apostle action was unholy including David, Moses but they came humble and repent and Jesus forgive them., Jacob run from his brother Esau before of the evil he do to him so Jacob went to country call bethel he and his people and right there he build an altar and call the place El bethel because it at that place God appear to him when he fled from his brother he receive the special gift of the Holy Ghost the second time God appear unto Jacob again when he came out of Paden Aram and bless Jacob after stealing from his brother, so God can bless the thief, the prostitute, the murder the cheat big But stop committed these crime like Jacob don't continue doing it or else Jesus will stop you no more presumptuous sin or doing sin habitual so here the promotion God gave scheming Jacob " Thy name is Jacob but thy name will no more call Jacob because it attached to bad thing but name change will be ISRAEL and declare himself saying I am GOD almighty he telling Jacob be fruitful, multiply a nation and a company of nation shall be of thee and kings shall come out of thy loin and the land which I gave ABRAHAM and Isaac I will also give to you and your generation and GOD went up from him in the place where he talk with Jacob and Jacob set up a pillar in that place where he talked with him even pillar of stone and Jacob pour out drink offering thereon and Jacob call that place where the great GOD talk with him "BETHEL"" what a conversation Jacob have with the living God. When last the living Jesus spoke with you answer this question? Yes, he speaks are listening or we are depending on preacher or prophets to tell what Jesus say, you can hear Jesus for yourself. Over 25 year in Jamaica I just got save and not even 2 week prior to be save true the shed blood of Jesus only one savior can save human kind is JESUS no other savior can save I was at work when Jesus appear to me and say :Daughter I need you to go on the high way, the bus and preach my Holy Spirit word it was me alone in the office so that voice was the original voice of Jesus it was not a pastor it Jesus, I wasn't in the temple, I wasn't with friends Jesus make sure I was alone so I would know it was the Savior and king Jesus. So yes Jesus speak to human Kind until 2020 present he still speaking, next encounter I was in new York over 2 year when Jesus himself and his voice came hovering over me about 4a.m in the morning speaking to me live and direct, this 2020 earlier in the year I sat in the car just finish pray and was waiting for JESUS to speak to me and tell what to do my boss, my husband Jesus Guess what Jesus come himself and say to me clearly "my daughter you are well protected and he have big umbrella covering me and then he show me so believer that was fighting against me" that encounter was specular if my phone was tune on I would take picture but when I waiting to hear his voice I turn off all noise and distraction.

And all my readers we must have a thankful heart at all times in our life whether in good time and bad time thank to Jesus don't depend on our situation thank must flow naturally like when we have the Holy Spirit and Jesus in our heart we love, we share, we have compassion for each other, we care for each other and respect each other whether they black, white, rich poor. Jesus must live in our heart not chain and tattoos or bumper on car with Jesus the important thing people must see the character of Jesus in us true us and don't have to wonder or these people Christian. Apostle David was worshiper, a fighter and always giving God thank even when the enemies surround him David would say "rejoice in the Lord ye righteous and give thanks at the remembrance of his holiness, before the Lord for he cometh for he cometh to judge the earth he shall judge the world with righteousness and the people with his truth David Psalm 97:12 I don't see no apostle can praise God Jesus but David and dance and he do with his hole heart, mind and soul he was committed and faithful to the living great God so don't hesitate start praise Jesus anywhere you are right now reading this book and thanking him for all his goodness in your personal life even if you are going true a hard time still thanks Jesus things will get better I challenge you in this 2020 and beyond. The Holy spirit that transform our life every day make sacrifice and get that super natural power, now Aaron and his sons was chosen of God to minister to the people of Israel but before they could minister Moses have to anoint, and consecrate them and they were fill with the Holy Spirit no preacher back in Israel or now present in 2020 can minister without having the Holy Spirit if you know anyone that is preaching or doing God work without the Holy Spirit they are not of Jesus they are the devil children if you read the Holy Bible you see for yourself that his Holy Spirit in us preaching God word it cannot be flesh or your own knowledge, God ordain Priest in those day to use the Olive oil as point of contact to anoint preacher, elders, members and surfaces including the temple, your families, your home and cars but these thing must be pray over by Jesus chosen people Moses make it an oil of holy ointment an ointment compound after the art of the apothecary it shall be an Holy anointing oil and thou shall anoint the tabernacle of the congregation and the ark of the testimony.. Genesis 30:29, Genesis Exodus 40:9 and Psalm 23:5 and Psalm 92:10 and Jesus' use water to heal and anoint, He use prayer cloth, he uses Sylvia to heal Rod Parsley Ministry big on using prayer cloth check out that ministry these are bible. I Claudia Henderson the author of this timely book uses the anointing Olive Oil every time I have a social media service or just preaching, I would have the olive oil and water because Jesus say I must use it not every preacher will use these things just who Jesus tell to do it. Just like Moses God have him use a ROD to bring in Egypt, Joshua use staff Jesus' gift is unique but is same result at the ends. So, the man God name Bezalel God fill with the Spirit of wisdom, understanding, knowledge all manner of workmanship for the silver smith to work with gold and silver the Holy Spirit give revelation knowledge Exodus 31:1 and 2.

Why some believer tarrying for the Holy Spirit and cannot receive it because we are still sinning lying, gossiping, having sex out of married, we are still hating each other, read Leviticus 19:16 to 18 don't eat anything with blood, no witchcraft, enchantment, make no cutting in your flesh, do not prostitute yourself or sell your body Christian less the land fill with whoredom and the land will with blood, no dirty envious heart Read it in Leviticus 19:26 to 31 no pride, no war Read it in Proverb 6:16 to the end God hate these evil bitterly. Jesus' pay is life for this church and we have to live Holy and please him not please people and do what people do else you will be cast out like the devil himself. So right now we are celebrating the DAY OF ATONEMENT in September of 2020 and every year September we celebrate this time when we ask Jesus for the forgiveness of our sin which I outline to you all it the HOLIEST time of the year just like we celebrate Christmas Jesus birth, and Easter Jesus resurrection it same way we must celebrate the day of atonement where we examine our life as Christian and start live Holy unto God so we can receive everything Jesus have for us and of course receive the Holy Spirit and talk with Jesus every day we must to be spiritual clean and physical clean and physiology clear and some of us believers stop gossiping people and examine our life. God tell Moses speak unto the Israelite and right now we are speaking to you people to celebrate tenth of seventh month there shall be a day of atonement, it will be a Holy Convocation unto to the Lord and we all must afflict our soul meaning pray unto the Lord for the sin you committed and bring an offering by fire at the altar at this solemn time do no work but fast and pray Leviticus 23:26 to 29 stop playing around Jesus and start get serious with him. So, after you atone for your sin here come jubilee of blowing the trumpet on the tenth day of the seven months in the season of the atonement it may true all the land and then return every man to his household Leviticus 25:9 to 13.

The result of empty ourself of sins things we do wrong resulting in God blessing in our life and families and friend because you are living Holy God spoke unto Moses and Aaron to bless the people of Israel saying to them " the Lord bless thee and keep thee some house say this blessing when you leaving the temple the blessing is popular the Lord make his face to shine on you all in 2020 and he his gracious unto us, the Lord lift up his countenance upon thee and give us peace we all need peace in this broken world, I can tell all my reader I sleep in my car for peace and the hotel because where I was living is so much war God Jesus give us everlasting peace so why are you choosing to live in war when you have a choice answer continue with this blessing and they shall put my name upon the children of Israel and God bless after the repentance and sacrifice make on the altar. You can make your altar anywhere you feel at peace to talk to Jesus it does matter read Number 6:22 to 27 for this popular blessing in 2020 we all need Jesus' blessing and approval. So, after the declaration of God blessing the children of Israel bring their tithes and offering to the altar the same altar they pray forgiveness and the princes offer for dedicating of the altar in that day when they give it was anointed even the official queen and prince give there tithes and offering and the content of the offering was silver charger the weight was heavy serious giving and they give gold and diamond the all put it on the altars read it all in number 7:10 to 15 and 26. The Holy Spirit transfer from Moses to 72 chosen man God chose to fight the enemies look they could go with Moses until they receive the Spirit of God here God command Moses to gather unto me seventy men of the elders of Israel whom knows to be the elders of the people and officers over them and bring them to the tabernacle of the congregation that they make stand there with Moses because the Holy Spirit on Moses is going to transfer to the these men and God say I God will talk to these chosen men before they do service watch this I will take the same Spirit which is on Moses and give it to them and they shall bear the burden of the people with Moses so God gave

Moses help to accomplish his work here on earth. Are as chosen people of God asking Jesus for help because we can't do alone Jesus did chose 12 apostles to help him my advice pray to Jesus to send you arm bearer and not doing on your own else you will live to regret it.

Now out of the thousands of Israelites that come out of Egypt including the leader Moses only 2 enter the paradise the promise land it really hard renders these people should it inherit want God to provide for them but they sin against God and complain and worship false God, peer pressure takes them over they start become people pleaser that be humble and obeying God so because of their action they never get the inheritance that was for them. Just like in the modern world in 2020 some of us miss out a good job because we are always late and just never do a good job, we always cheating on your wife and husband and don't want to stop until we lose the love of our life, we are gossiping and noses in people business and then people start disrespecting us because of our action we always busy and never spent time in the presence of God so we can't really get the blessing of God for what it worth that the same way with these Israelite. The two that get the paradise is Caleb and Joshua because they have the right kind of Jesus Spirit Hear the recommendation God gave Caleb " but my servant Caleb because he had another Spirit with him and had follow me God fully him will I bring in the land where he go and his seed meaning all his generation with inherit and possess this land" so all my reader when you please the creator of the university you are in line for your blessing even if you don't please mother, father, husband, wife, children, pastor, believers it very important you please God. But try to live in peace with everyone including the enemies don't take revenge but pray and forgive your enemies Jesus say I will repay all those who abuse and hurt you and learn to forgive and forget even if they want to kill you. When they abuse JESUS and before they kill him second to last word, he says father God forgive because they don't know what they done Jesus and Job been true hard trial that no apostle in the bible been true and yet still they forgive all their enemies so do the same out there. I see people come against me for nothing just plain envy and hate and I pray for them every day even present 2020 and some of these enemies are disease now some are suffering because I never take revenge Jesus do it., he fight for David, he fight for Moses, he fight for Gideon , he fight for sister Claudia and Jesus is fighting for you call you name and say Jesus is fighting for Jody, Delray, vie, dick, tom and harry right pause and call you name before the living God and say Jesus is fighting every poverty, every sickness including corona virus, cancer, diabetes, every street and depression every sin right now he is fighter lay.. every weapon you have now and let Jesus that won the devil fight for you amen glory. Read number 14 all of it to get the full meaning some of the Israelite start fighting against Moses they became jealous and envious because God was using Moses mightily just in your life when you are anointed of God or get rich, or get married and even get a promotion they some people will not celebrate you because they are e envious of you it the same with the apostle Moses Korah and his man rose up against Moses saying the enemies speaking "ye take too much upon you seeing all the congregation are holy every one of them and the Lord is among you wherefore then lift ye up yourselves above the congregation of the lord" And when Moses hear the enemies speak he went and start pray to and Moses say to the enemies the Lord will judge between me on you tomorrow and God destroy the enemies and same is chosen man Moses. Look how Moses approach this problem in prayer that how God children operate no cursing, no fighting but pray read it in number 16 from 1 to 22. When we believers have a problem, we should not go to the court of law we should get the pastor or the priest and pray about it and settle it and this is biblical.

Moses fill with the Spirit of God tell all the Israelite and we are telling you now in 2020 century know this day and consider in our heart that the Lord is our God in heaven above and under beneath there no other God but our true God that creature all things and other duty as believers to is to keep his statutes and his commandment where he wrote in Exodus 20 that your days is prolong upon the face of the earth., we as Christian that have a relationship with God must do these commandment every day and not do what we feel like is right in our eyes. And God continue to show us is glory true sign, wonder, true speak to us verbally and true prophets and dream that how is glory is manifested read it in Deuteronomy 5:24 Being in contact with the heavenly team will bring success and fulfillment for your personal life when we obey Jesus covenant and commandment look what you get from the master ":and he will love thee and bless thee and increase thee daily he will bless the fruit of our womb like Abraham wife Sarah at 90 year old Sarah have baby it not time or space it God time so be hopeful and keep believing and the fruit of thy land they corn, thy wine and the oil and everything we put our hand will be bless so stop waiting for people to bless it may never happen look to the creator for you blessing., and God blessing will promote us of all the people on the earth receive this blessing in your spirit and stop saying if it for you and somebody else, yes it for you I don't care who you are poor, rich, black or white it for you read it in Deuteronomy 7:12 to 15 that your will to inherit before you die and read Deuteronomy 11:26 and 27 it not every believer including prophets have the Holy Spirit because some of them use satanic spirit the bible say try every Spirit because some of these spirit of God., warning on false preacher, teacher and preachers if there arise among you a prophets or a dreamer of dream and give you sign of a wonder and the sign of the wonder come pass whereof he speak unto you let us go after other false God which you have not known and want you to serve them thou should hearken unto word of that false prophets it a warning from God, Satan was God right hand man so he also know the word he right there so search all the Spirit and Jesus will tell you right Spirit read Deuteronomy 13:1 to 5 this Holy word was written thousands of year ago and all in the bible is happening now in this world the plaque in Egypt is happening now in form of corona virus, we see tornado, hurricane, we see people dying from all sought of disaster it was predict year ago before it happen so this bible cannot lie God is not a liar. I mention early in this book when Christian have a matter we not supposed to go to the earthly judge we must go to the pastor or priest and let them resolve it read Deuteronomy 17:8 to 12 we cannot function like non-Christian meaning sinner he have to operate like God chosen people meaning we cannot murder, gossiping, cheat that what sinner do for the Lord chosen us out of all the tribe to stand to minister in the name of the Lord and our generation., anywhere God have us minister we shall do abomination of those nations separate yourself from demonic people on preach Jesus word to them but don't keep friends with them is a warning Deuteronomy 18:1 to 16 this great way for reading the bible.

So when God send you a prophet listen and do what the prophet say as long as God send them the Lord will raise up a prophet from the midst of our people and do what the prophet say, the blessing assurance of the Lord that he will avouched us this day to be a special people that live on is earth and make us high above all nation which he had made in praise, and in name, and in honor and we in turn must be a holy people unto the lord God spoken it Deuteronomy 26:16 to 19 read all the blessing God have for us and make sure you get them but these blessing have condition all these blessing shall come on thee and overtake you "if thou shall heaven unto the voice of the Lord " bless thou shall be in city and all over world anywhere you shall go it will Jesus blessing overtake you people must want what we have not what they have that the real blessing, one of my spiritual father name VT Williams preach to us couple year in Jamaica blessing must run us down if we are connected to Jesus. Blessing shall be the fruit of our body meaning good health not just money alone and the fruit of the ground and the fruit of all livestock, bless shall be in our store house so we can give to anyone who need these blessing. So we see the Holy Spirit on Moses transfer to Joshua because Moses was about go and we always need back up and Joshua was full of the Spirit of wisdom and Moses lay is hand on Joshua and the Spirit of the transfer to Joshua reader you see the transfer of the Holy Spirit., Moses encourage Joshua say "be strong and very courageous so you can do all that left to continue so everyone don't give up but keep press on if Jesus approve you to do it the greatest approval come from God not man, when I was preaching in my earlier year some pastor, members tell God never chose me but I follow what Jesus ask me to do and not what pastor say and member because they are not God, people you got to realize it not all preacher hearing from God they are religious leader like the Pharisee and scribe when you have a relationship you will see for yourself. So, you see how God exalt and promote Joshua in the midst of all people after he take over from Moses make sure your approval and confirmation come from Jesus not man the second appointment is pastor, look at the next encounter Joshua have for the second time there was angel over

Joshua confirming his call and immediately Joshua humble fell on the ground and worship God that how humble we have to been as man and women of God Joshua 5:13 to 15. I preach all the time when God confirm don't worry of people approval just be respectful listen their feedback good or bad. When our life hangs on people approval, we are in serious trouble you will never hear from God, because he needs us to be is main source of survival not job, or husband or wife. I hope we are thank God anywhere we are known and stop complaining and gossiping there is blessing in praise and thank giving reader now the transfer of the Holy Spirit from Joshua to a next prophet name Othniel to bring on the good work and the Holy spirit came on him and is job was to judge the children of Israel and he won all the enemies because the Holy Spirit was in him true him judges 3:10 and then the Holy Spirit transfer to Judge Deborah prophetess and mother of Israel of she did a perfect job destroying all the enemies not because of their own strength but because the power was in them to do their job., and we travelling with the Holy Spirit and I know you are there with me before this book end if you don't have the Holy Spirit you will get it when you finish read it because every born again Christian should have it and leave the flesh alone that why some temple are empty because the power of God is not there so people left, we out witnessing so much complain that church people and pastor are boring and the dry because there is no Holy Spirit. Next man of God that get the Holy Spirit is Gideon was chosen he just sat under an oak tree when the angel appears to him that God chose him to rescue the people of Israel, so some believers think that is all the time pastors chose you know the pick is when Jesus chose you Judges 6:11 to 17 and when Gideon get call he pray and won all the enemies.

It very important I tell the Body of Christ that all believers need the Holy Spirit so I look for man and women of God that he chose and fill be they do is service the next prophet was Jephthah was fill with the Holy Spirit and right he vowed unto God that he deliver all the enemies into is hand and free up the children in care of the Holy Spirit we won all because of the Holy Spirit and our obedient to God, every one that read and study the bible read and know of samson story he was the strongest man back there in Israel because of the Holy Spirit he won most of enemies but in the last enemies defeat because samson never obey God rule. You see to have the Holy Spirit is one, but we have to obey what he tells us to do that make us a champion both go hand in hand just like faith have to go with work for example it takes to people to married not one is the same with the Holy Spirit. get this in your spirit. Next prophets are Saul when Samuel appoint Saul this time God tell Samuel to appoint Saul some time God tell the real Holy Spirit to appoint elder, prophets is not all the time Jesus will come himself and the Spirit of the Lord will come upon thee and thou shall prophesy we got to have the Spirit to preach and prophesy not just bible knowledge but Holy Spirit first and then bible school but still go to the bible school, make sure you are fill with the Holy Spirit. I know so temple you can take part until you are fill with the Holy Spirit and that the right way that how Jesus do business in the kingdom of God, he would never let the apostle teach or preach until they all receive the infilling of the Holy Spirit, so those pastors are so right. 1 Samuel 10:4 to 5 but just like samson King Saul sin against God and he take back the Holy Spirit and I evil spirit take over King Saul read Saul confession and that could be some you out there confession 1 Samuel 13:11 to 13 so because Saul lose out on God he send the same prophet Samuel to let David take it over just like you fail at your job the boss fire you get someone else to work is same thing with Saul and David so you understand clearly what we are saying here, so Samuel go to David house and anoint David with the oil and anoint David in the midst of his family and brethren and after such a lovely anoint ceremony the Special Spirit fill David same spirit Saul have. 1 Samuel 16:12 to 14 there was wizard man in the bible try to buy the Holy Spirit from the Apostle but Paul rebuke and tell only Jesus can give this power not even a trillion dollar can buy this Holy Spirit, just like a good male or female you will never sell your sex even if someone offer a trillion dollar because you know true love cannot be brought on Jesus give you true love is same thing with the only spirit can be buy or share you have to have your original portion. After David receive the Holy Spirit, he behaves himself wisely in all his ways and the Lord was with him when Saul saw David behave, he was afraid of David and all Judah and Israel love David because he was humble and gentle. Saul gets envious of David and want to hurt David he got jealous of David anoint just like some of us out there we get all the chance out there in life and loose it and then we want to blame someone for our action. So, when Saul sends messenger to take out David, but the messenger saw the prophets prophesying Samuel standing as appointed over them the Holy Spirit was transfer to them and they also prophesying that powerful get around Holy Spirit people and final you will have it when you are around winner you start win opposite when you around loser you become one so be careful who you hang around. everyone Saul sends set the Holy Spirit 1 Samuel 19:20 to 21 he sends them to hurt David, but God never allow nothing to happen to his chosen.

Now Saul was so upset with David he vowed to destroy David, but he got away from him to avoid trouble just like some us we do anything to have quiet life is same with David they were hiding out in the same cave and David hold his garment and could have easily kill Saul but David stays faithful to God. Saul confesses to David saying "I sinned I will not no more arm you because my soul was precious in thy sight behold, I have played the fool and wrong exceedingly 1 Samuel 26:21 to 24. I remember in this 2020 someone do me wrong and God allow her to apologize to me A lot of who hurt you and do you wrong will apologize like Saul to David may sure you forgive all your haters and enemies. Now when God stop talking to you because of your sin look what happen from King Saul hunter of the night seeking someone to tell what to do he went to seir woman that have familiar spirit meaning witches, palm reader the King disguise himself because he never want nobody see him just like us out there some movie star or famous people disguise themselves to be out there because they don't want any amusement, but by Saul surprise the witch women say Saul by tomorrow you will be in the grave that is lost resort and yes Saul die in battle the enemies he should won kill him, why he lost because the power of the Holy Spirit left him God stop speaking to him so he lost. Some of these preachers start with Jesus like Saul and let the devil finish them in offer them big money and they could help themselves their greed and flesh let them take it and now they are working for the devil not God I as defender and preacher of God word or ashamed of some of these preachers I stop watch them because things they are doing now in 2020 is not of Jesus when you have a relationship with Jesus you know some of them change like Saul. So, take finally become the new King of Israel and won most of his battle because Jesus was with him and he walk with obedient and humble do the same like King David., I love David story of perfect obedient, humble and uniqueness every Christian should read 1 and 2 Samuel and all his psalm and David's son Solomon take over from David when he was old the Holy Spirit on Solomon was the wisest man on earth because he please the lord like is father David. David could not build the temple so is son build the most expensive temple of all time millions of dollar guess who appear in the temple at the mercy seat? God in thick cloud because of those faith fill prayer every time when Jesus appear is at the mercy seat nowhere else but the mercy seat CeCe winna sing song name mercy say no meaning when we are guilty Jesus mercy say no and it came to pass when the priest were come out of the Holy Place " the cloud fill the and God glory fill the house, when the last time God Glory fill you temple, I saw I pastor was talking about one day in a dream Jesus bring on his back and show so unholy act that was happening in the temple evil stuff that so false preacher committed the pastor say it was horrible and it true. I go to church all over and I saw it with my spiritual eyes and my naked eye I was alarm that so of these believers do resend God house that why their temple is getting empty every day because it there flesh it not the true Holy Spirit be careful of false prophets and prophetess, I am warning you. The Lord told Solomon before he come that he would dwell in the thick cloud in the temple just like somebody coming over to your house they let you know before they come it same way with our Great God of manner and respect. 1 King 8:11 to 16 read this scripture I am giving you.

We need to get very deep in the Holy Spirit and the relevant to our life in the 2020 century it still relevant now no miracle can wrath without the Holy Spirit Prophet Jehu got and also won the enemies and Elijah and Elisha got and was great do exploit for God glory so hear the prophet Elijah say to Israelite if God be God serve him and if Baal be Baal serve him you see people Jesus give us choices from day one chose this day who you will serve, my advice is the Baal devil come to kill steal and destroy now our High Priest come to give live and more abundantly chose right now who you going to serve. So there was an evil Woman and his Evil husband name Jezebel and Ahab they were false teacher of God word and let Israel sin against God because of their false idolatry just like in this world we have a lot false preacher I mention it early became there first sin was covetousness of the man vineyard like you have house and some envious of the house you have it say way in Israel her second major evil was Slew God Prophets and hide her crime we would say she cover it so nobody would see but we can't hide from God. Guess what God raise up a prophet Elijah fill with the Holy Ghost and send him to Jezebel let her know tomorrow this time like king Saul your body will the fowls eat she forget the Great God was watching her evil and has the prophets say she die disgraceful Jezebel because she kills God Chosen are some of us like jezebel pretending to be save and when we left the sanctuary, we are doing evil answer your question? Read it in 1 king 21:18 to 29 see the judgment of the living God so don't take revenge let Jesus fight your battle., next chosen prophet one of favor is Jehoshaphat chosen also of God and fill with the Spirit of God but was surrounded by enemies when he look on the amount of enemies he go to the temple and pray to the Lord the Lord him say just set up the praise team and worship notice all of the chosen men and women of God never use gun, knife or no form of weapon just praise, praise and reading the word with the Holy Spirit and important obey. The King Jehoshua won victoriously amen So God take up the Prophet Elijah because he was zealous and fill with the Spirit of God was on was taken up in heaven alive so you know some believers will go to heaven alive without dying the Spirit of Elijah go into Elisha Spirit transfer to the other prophets so when he receive the Spirit the people came and meet him and bow before him 2 kings 2:14 to 16 and heal the are water and then heal the women daughter and heal Naaman the leprosy give up for the prophets and prophetess that represent God in all way. The prophet Jehu kill the false Baal prophets of the devil and burn it with fire jehu destroy Baal out of Israel and Jezebel was destroy read 2 kings 9:33 to 37 and 2 kings 10:26 to 28 the devil strong hold burns down completely so you can start get devil out of your life right now if you apply God rule to fight this war let Jesus lead you. The Holy Spirit that bring the dead to life the Prophet Elisha die and bury and they bring a dead man to bury in Elisha grave they knew know somebody bury there because it was just pure bone the put the man into the sepulcher of Elisha and when the man was let down and touch the bone of Elisha he came to live meaning dead touching dead because the Holy Spirit was still alive even dough Elisha God chosen prophet was dead that the super natural God we serve the greatest Doctor is name Jesus Jehovah orphan our healing read it in 2 king 13:20 to 21 only believe all thing are possible when you believe out there.

The Holy Spirit give us real top blessing there was man in the bible name Jabez his mother bear him in pain and sorrow just like some mother can relate to Jabez mother but when he was born God appear unto him like Solomon and ask brother Jabez what can I do for you like how he as Solomon, Jabez was more honorable that all his brethren just like when Moses was born they hide because he was proper child is same like Jabez requested 'O lord that thou would bless me indeed and enlarge my coast and thine hand will always be with me Jabez and that thou would protect and keep me from evil that I may not grieve thee and the GREAT GOD GRANT JABEX IS REQUEST" so keep asking Jesus for what you need never give up even if it days, weeks and year keep pursuing and have faith in Jesus never give up on Jesus. I am a partner of Trinity Broadcasting New {TBN} television from Paul and Jen couch day and Paul talk of how God Jesus literally save TBN miraculous because they never have all the money but from nowhere Jesus send I religion man to save TBN now we have TBN for over 40 year, he may not come when we want but he will never let us go over the precept so don't throw in towel and give up stay in line even if you are at the back of the line wait your turn we soon come to the front say God. I personal be true a lot too you see the first chapter of my "MY MESS BECOME OUR MESSAGE OF LOVE" if I never being true the trial and problems, I never really know my Jesus is the miracle worker he is in my personal life., all my problem is not over but just like you keep praying every day and have faith in God. King David take over the throne and look the Holy Spirit in David transfer to his arm bearer captain and David receive them and work with them, arm bearer must have the same Spirit and be in unity if we are not united we cannot achieve nothing in the kingdom of

God no division any problems sought out before the people find out 1 chronicles 12:18 David get famous because of the Holy Spirit all nation start to honor him because of Jesus just like Michael Jackson, Whitney Houston and Elvis Presley it even more honor amen to the Lamb. Surprise David give his son Solomon the House of God must build by the Spirit in this world before you build the house you have to a blue print be construction started well the Holy Spirit was the blue print for the temple interested, I really amaze how the detail of the Holy Spirit operate. The Spirit of God fill the Prophet Azariah and he make peace with the People of Israel and they put away the idol from them and start to worship the living God that what God Spirit do let us live Holy and pure. There is no man on earth have power over the Holy Spirit to retain the Spirit neither in the day of death there is no discharge in that war, neither shall wickedness deliver those that are given to it only God can control the Spirit of life, The Holy Spirit shall rest on his chosen people Spirit of Wisdom and understanding, the Spirit of counsel and might, the Spirit of knowledge and of the Lord, do you have these aspect of Holy Spirit make sure we have all not just some section of the Holy Spirit it must be excellent in all part and have the Spirit of Truth when the Holy Spirit pour in us the right way we are fruitful bear good friend in term of winning soul for God kingdom, lay hand on the sick and they are heal, we see the blessing in finance, family and good health that end product of the Holy Spirit we are bless in every area of our life not just some. 32:15. The prophet Isaiah when he was in the Spirit and saw Jesus before he was born high and lifted up and his trail fill the temple and also weeping prophets Jeremiah was also in the Spirit to speak to backslidden Israel of what should happen. God call the rejected women she was grief in the Spirit and I wife of youth but she was chosen by God even doth rejected by people she was chosen so if you are out there and rejected by your own that okay Jesus embrace you with wide open arm and you are safe.

Now God make a covenant with us is chosen this covenant is present effective for 2020 the Spirit that is upon us speak the Holy Spirit which was place in our mouth it shall not depart nor from our generation but speak the life Holy Spirit to everyone you see and don't speak Satan language of gossiping and lying and cursing bottom line speak God word and send satanic packing back to his house hell and doom. Isaiah 59:21. When the Spirit of Truth in us it shall teach us everything we need to know about God, Jesus that the job of the Holy Spirit gives us revelation knowledge, wisdom and understand so no Christian must take part in gossip news because the Holy Spirit will tell you everything you need to know, Christian must be Holy in all way not just some way but all. Jesus was one hundred percent man and one hundred percent God and he was pure and Holy, tested life us in all way and never fail so we can do it. Look what revolutionize the Body of Christ the Holy Spirit here what the prophet Isaiah says: "The Spirit of the Lord is upon me because he hath anointed me to preach we have to have the Spirit to preach, prophesy, pray, teach and sing everything we do in the Body of Christ it must have to be motivated by the Holy Spirit good tiding unto the meek, Jesus send us bind the broken hearted to proclaim liberty to the captives and the opening of the prison to them that are bound, to proclaim the acceptable year of the Lord and the day of vengeance of our God; to comfort all that mourn" Isaiah 61:1 and 2 so all my reader and believers you see what we believer should be doing preach to loss, lay our hand on the sick and they recover, see prosperity to all believers first are we seeing these thing happening in where you worship, if don't it time to pray about going where the Spirit fill church. Without the Spirit we are like dead and dry and boring, but the Spirit give life and life most abundant. The youngest of all the prophets were Jeremiah when God call Jeremiah he was about 5 year old that when Jeremiah hear the voice of God he reply say "I am little boy and I can't speak" but God say "I will put the Holy SPIRIT word in your mouth to speak to backslidden Israel Jesus continue to speak to Jeremiah say "before I form you in your mother womb I knew you Jeremiah and sanctify thee and ordained the a Prophets unto the nations of the world, what confident God gave Jeremiah and right now in 2020 Jesus is calling some of you are you heeding to the call be obedient and to what the Master tell you to do, this is opportunity of your life many are call but few are chosen make sure you are in the chosen not the many. When we have the Jesus Spirit, we fight against the false spirit without we even knowing amen some prophets prophesy falsely and some priest bear rule by their means. Therefore, pray not thou these people neither lift up nor pray for them, neither make intercession for them because I Jesus will not hear and answer them., Jeremiah 7:16 so Jesus is saying there are some people that do me wrong and I just not going to brother with them that it? When Jesus finish with you it done and over, when your wife, husband, children, co-worker or finish with you that okay but when Jesus' finish with you is done like the dead in the grave. Why Jesus not hearing your prayer and supplication because of evil in is sight do abominable thing in God house and pollute it and they build the high places of Baal and burn incense and sacrifice their son and daughter to the devil these evil upset God so out there make sure we are obeying Jesus so he can be pleased with our action and word., some of these pastors and believers have become brutish and stray for the Lord we are telling why some prayer don't answer and cause the member to leave and go astray Jeremiah 10:21 and Jeremiah 11:14 and Jeremiah 12:10 we as Christian need to get it right in 2020 and beyond.. Jeremiah 14:14 to 16.

The Spirit of the living God bring restoration and resurrection life back there in Israel sin bad against God and he destroy of the earth in is wrath, just like some us when someone did us bad, we tense to want to fight back because we are hurt well that how we upset God with murder, stealing, lying, gossiping and we need to stop doing evil. So God raise up the prophet Ezekiel to go where those dead body was oh yes and prophesy unto those dead bone and Ezekiel go because I God will cause breath to blow back in them and sinews upon them and put back flesh upon you and we shall know that I am great God., look on God mercy in action it does matter how bad thing get just keep believing that restoration is coming for you and your family all we preach, pray, sing it bold down to BELIEVE that you shall Raise again like the people in Israel Jesus is still the same miracle worker you can trust God. The Holy Spirit is transferring to people, prophets, members, pastor and whoever need and believe this Holy Spirit so the Prophet Daniel was in exile where it was mostly enemies because they were taken away captive but Daniel show everyone that there still Great God that he serve and he show the enemies the character of Jesus and he was favor by the King because he portrait holiness and he was prefer about all the princes, because an excellent Spirit was in him and the king set Daniel over the whole kingdom because of the Spirit in him so try get the God Spirit not the satanic Spirit. The Spirit that overflowing to all people now is time of getting this Holy Spirit Joel say " it will come to pass that I God that give the Spirit will pouring out to all flesh and your son and daughter, your mother, father will prophesy and you will see the Lord and dream vision of heaven because of the Holy Spirit Joel 2:28 to 32 if you don't have the Holy Spirit reading this timely book before you finish read this book you will be fill with the Holy Spirit only believe and don't care your religion just and have a relationship with Jesus so you can be fill with the Holy Spirit. The Holy Spirit building and giving us the spiritual blue print and detail of the foundation and the Lord stirred up the Spirit of Zerubbabel governor of Judah, and the Spirit of Joshua the high priest and the Spirit of remnant of the people and they all came and did work in the house of the Lord our God so all these different Spirit came together and the result is work they build the temple of God Haggy 1:14 The Spirit that destroy the enemies out of your life everyone should need the Holy Spirit to do great things you will overthrow the throne of the heathen and there chariots and the sword of their ancestor nothing shall left of them all the property will go, the sickness will go everyone that the devil have to fight against you will be history because Jesus is fighting for us every day all day because we are God prize possession and he defend us always. It not by might or by Power but by the Spirit say the Lord Zechariah 4:6. In the last day God will send us Elijah the prophets before the coming of lord he will turn the heart of the father to the children and the heart of all people back to God. We see the Conception of Jesus the seed was of the Holy Ghost we all are beneficiary of the Holy Ghost that the DNA of the children of God the Holy Ghost Matthew 1:18 when JESUS was adult and baptize after he was led in the Spirit to pray for forty night and day so that why prayer is effective because of the Holy Spirit Matthew 3:16 so after the advance prayer and fasting he went into their synagogues preaching the glorious gospel of his Father God and healing all manner of diseases, you see the process

1. From the birth it was Spirit
2. Baptize in the Holy Spirit
3. Preach, teach healing the sick because is driving force was the HOLY SPIRIT.

So, if we are serving Jesus and disciples, members, pastor, singer etc. how we don't have this Power source we need to get this Special Holy Spirit to do great thing for Jesus. Look at the result lot of people start following Jesus because of miracles they see and hear so is fame start televise all over the world until present.

Look at Jesus teaching he speak with Power and authority not as false teacher and preachers hear what our High Priest say "Jesus opens his mouth and taught the people blessed are the poor in Spirit for there is the kingdom of God the first lesson he tells is the Holy Spirit read all in Matthew 5 all of Jesus teaching and he say we must love our enemies and pray for them that hurt us and despiteful use us and forgive them all. The only sin Jesus don't forgive is "when you sin against the HOLY SPIRIT" wherefore I Jesus say unto you all manner of sin and blasphemy shall be forgiven mean when you lie, steal, murder, cheat you will be forgiven: but when your blasphemy against the HOLY SPIRIT you will never get forgiveness Matthew 12:31 when you Sin against Jesus and God you will forgive but when you sin against the HOLY SPIRIT you will not get fogginess. You see how special this Holy Spirit start value this treasure gift from God and start treat more than trillion dollars., this long teaching but you will see the important of the Holy Spirit, Love, faith and obedient in the Kingdom of God. The Holy Spirit and the Love of God have us going to the highways, the prison, jail, banging on door, outreach in the public transportation and different county and states because the Holy Spirit stir us up Matthew 22:9 and 10 the Spirit of Love true love beyond our control meaning you can love people society cast off, we can love the reject, we can love in spite of status are race when they ask Jesus what the greatest commandment Jesus answer back " thou shall love the Lord with all they heart and soul and love your enemies and Jesus was talking about sex that he was talking is giving, sharing, preaching our father word the Spirt is God living our heart every day we house the super natural we are the contain of God walking here on earth. The Holy Spirit that generate praise and worship to roof this women was a sinner she done a lot of evil in her life but she value Jesus than some of us believers she bring the most expensive ointment to anoint the messiah do you Christian really value Jesus that much that you pray every day, worship every day, obey Jesus every day, live Holy every day and share and give every day that value Jesus in our action not our word this women even won over is disciples because some of his disciple say why you are using such expensive oil and Jesus because they never value him to that extend, but this women place value on Jesus and guess what Jesus say to her and is apostles "wheresoever this gospel shall be preach in this whole world is because of the good work this sinful women have done in memory of her. This woman was not even a Christian but she knows that Jesus was very special to him and she left the present of Jesus very much save and change Matthew 26:1 to 12 the bible says if my people to serve and worship me I will let the rock cry out and worship me so don't let the rock cry out to Jesus when you have mouth and voice to worship. Noah was preacher of righteousness and preach for quite a while and the stubborn people never give there soul over the God and when he prepare a ark for those who are ready the people left to perish and animal take the place of people so don't let it happen to you out there, now you hear the gospel on television, radio, at the house of God, on Social media, on the bus and train all over so heed to Jesus before it too late, I Claudia Henderson the author of this timely book have Facebook service every Sunday at 3pm USA time and everyone is free to listen and watch God word preach, because when Jesus come we have to be ready we can't be preparing but "ready". When they put Jesus on the cross it was lot of pain but look at this the last word Jesus say before the die was "God I return back your Spirit" meaning the Spirit Jesus have he know when he dies the Spirit cannot be use, so when you don't have the Spirit in your body you are like dead living and breathing but dead spiritual.

So on the 3 day Jesus rose from the dead because God gave him back the Holy Spirit that raise in back to live and was see by Mary and his disciples and then other people alive now before Jesus went back to our father God to his disciple saying "all power is given unto you all in heaven and earth Jesus commission his disciple to teach all nation, baptizing them in the name of the Father, Son and Holy Ghost now here is Holy Ghost again in action and alive teaching them to observe all things where I command them to go and lo I Jesus is with us until present 2020 so you are not alone members, pastor, prophets, evangelist, singer we are not alone. We see the baby John too was conceive of Holy Ghost john is one that baptize Jesus so you see the connection 2 babies have the Holy Ghost Luke 1 v 15 and John fill with the Holy Spirit was preaching the repentance message of hope and Love and many people was save. This pastor from the USA go to Pakistan this county is mostly Muslim these people believe in different savior name all but the Holy Spirit was on this pastor and go and preach to these people and tens of thousands of Muslims got save and leave their false religion on right now serving the true savior Jesus. We have to have the Spirit of truth to do great thing for Jesus pull strong hold that no false prophets or teacher can do when I see the video on face body this is Jesus with working of the Holy Spirit in action do God way and stop fake it. In this present world people know when you are faking it to make and lady get fire because she was faking it to make be real be God true original handmade and you will truly make big. He that hungry and thirsty after Holiness will be fill, Jacob the patriarch was tired of doing evil but one day he decides I am going to pray to Jesus until all these guilt and shame go and he stay with God until he was totally free, sometime we ask Jesus to forgive of the things we do wrong but we know we are not totally free something nagging us every time is like somebody torturing us. So that how we have to tarry until we really and truly receive the Holy Spirit it does matter if we are uncomfortably Holy Spirit is must have for all believers in the globally Body of Christ. When we are preaching and praying without the Holy Spirit, we are false be careful of false Christ and false prophets they shall rise and show sign like they are real and wonder to seduce us down these false preachers will operate especially in the last days and we are seeing some of them operating right now in the present world but don't give him and don't serve them be watchful and be on the alert. When the Spirit of God came on Jesus, he was full and ready to do the work of the master, and he close the book and gave it to the minister and sat in the temple and all eyes was upon him because the real savior has come to silent all the false one. When you are in trouble or in s situation say nothing until the Holy Spirit will tell what to say and obey and say it don't say thing on your own else you will get deeper into more trouble., and the Holy Spirit give us comfort when we really need it especially know when we have so much going on when Jesus was leaving earth he tell his disciples the comforter which is the Holy Spirit whom the father will send in my name will teach us all thing and bring all things in remembrance which I tell you, so we see the Holy spirit teaching us all truth and guide us. The Holy Spirit give commandment who he has chosen for Jesus say to the apostle's apostle John baptize you with water but I Jesus will baptize you with the Holy Ghost on fire, the power of Holy Spirit is different aspect of the Holy Spirit that make us be effective witness everywhere we witness. The Unity of the Holy Spirit we have to be on one accord in anticipation to receive this Holy Spirit when Jesus left the disciple was on one accord in unit at the upper room and they were in prayer to receive this power and the day finally arrive Pentecost come they were in oneness and suddenly there came a sound from heaven as rushing mighty wind it fill the house they were what an experience do you remember how you receive this Holy Spirit and how you were save we should treasure these moment like when you marry, or your birthday or graduation.. the Holy come with cloven tongues like as fire and each of the apostle receive the infilling of the Holy Spirit and they speak with other tongues that gave them utterance. So, we have to do it God way not the world way read act 1:8 to 11 and act 1:14 Act 2:1 to 5.

So, after the remanding Apostle receive the Holy Spirit then they start go out to preach and pray for the people and healing them because of the Holy spirit and lot people got save. Continue in the Spirit that turn the witches to Jesus Evangelist Phillip was God preacher at that time and he preach the word of God but in Samaria there was evil man name Simon that use divination, sorcery and bewitched the people of the city, just like some place you go there is palm reader, illuminate, witches that represent the devil it same thing with this evil man but when the real man of God go in the city this evil man name Simon believe and was save by the blood of Jesus, so you see the great power of the Holy Spirit take down the devil territory and destroy it. The Next evil man was Saul that was fighting against God people and one day Jesus contract and say "Saul why persecutes thou me" and for three day he was blind until Jesus send his servant to pray for him and he receive back is sight and was one of the greatest apostle in the body of Christ from Saul to change of name because of the bad reputation he has God give him a new name, name nature Apostle Paul that write most of the New testament what a transformation and the Jesus can do it for you if you let him from murder to be Holy and pure, from a lying to start talk the truth, from whore to be descent Lady that the change Paul receive from the lord and he his reaching out to you situation he giving us beauty for ashes you are not condemn it does matter the pass you have. So, Apostle Paul ministry take-off be of the transformation he receives and fill with the Holy Spirit everywhere he preaches soul are save people are heal because he is fully into Jesus full time, he was false Christian when he was doing those evil yes, he was because he never has this relation with Jesus, but when he receives the in filling of the Holy Spirit, he starts operate in rightness the churches established in the faith and more people added every day. Act 16:5 So Paul next assignment was to destroy all false God that not of the faith there was witch women name Dania but Paul defeats these Godless women and set her kingdom and ought that our assignment as man and women of God to win the devil every time he approaches by tempting us with flesh, money and thing that not of Jesus tell them no Jesus will give us the thing we need okay to fall in the devil trap you will live to regret it. Now as Paul witness the great gospel of Jesus in different country and cities he says "now I am bound in the Spirit unto Jerusalem knowing the thing that should be fall me save the Holy Ghost so Paul flow in the Spirit in good time and bad time is still the Spirit you know thing before it happens that the job of the Holy Spirit. There is no condemnation to us all that are in Christ Jesus because walk not after the sinful flesh but we walk according to the Spirt the Spirit set us free from the law and gave us liberty true the Spirit meaning the Spirit gave mercy when we are guilty thank Jesus for this Holy Spirit that bring us peace. So, if any believers have not the Holy Spirit been not of God read it in Roman 8:9 when we are let by the Spirit of God, we are son and daughter of the highest God. We have not received the bondage Spirit but we receive the adoption wherein we cry abba father the Spirit itself bearish witness with our Spirit that we are the children of God the first fruit of the Lord.

So, we all ministers of Jesus Christ to the non-believers preach the word of God so it may be acceptable and sanctified by the Holy Spirit that show mighty sign and wonder to them and pray in the Holy Spirit. Now we preacher and teacher of the word must pattern Paul humble he say this powerful "I came not to you with excellency of speech or of wisdom declaring unto you all the testimony of God but preach save Jesus Christ crucified but in demonstration of the Spirit of Power 1 Corinthians 2:1 to 4. So, the secrets of God that he hides from so much people he reveals true the Spirit of God especially the deep thing of God so you need to hear this hidden secret try and get the Holy Spirit so you will see and know Corinthians 2:7 to 12. When to the Lord we become partner in the Spirit our body is the temple of the Lord and the Holy Spirit so we must glorify God in our body and in the Spirit which are God. The different gift the Holy Spirit give and it bear good fruit when the Spirit give wisdom, word of knowledge, faith, healing, working of miracles, prophecy, discerning of Spirit, tongue, interpretation of tongue so you see clearly is the Spirit of God give these awesome gift 1 Corinthians 12 from 1 to 11 which gift Jesus gave you and are you using these gift are hiding it? my advice use these gift to the glory of Jesus name so is Kingdom will be establish here on earth and he get the glory. When you are in the house of God when you speaking in tongue make sure you have an interpreter as the Spirit gave utterance when you are at home you don't need an interpreter but Jesus but only in public you need an interpreter 1 Corinthians 14:13 to 17 so Jesus prefers in the temple, we prophesy that speak in tongue even the Apostle Paul would not leave until he gets Pentecost because that make the way for great ministry Pentecost, that the seal of approval the Holy Spirit. When you going true the airport there have to be seal that you can travel to different county if you don't have that seal you cannot travel is the same with the Holy Spirit it what seal to know we are children of God. I was preaching on social media I tell the people our language as believer is the Holy Spirit, love, peace, caring and sharing that God Seal. So, we see the Spirit give freedom where the spirit of the Lord is there is indeed liberty and let us pull down strong hold. Father Abraham was the blessing faith father of us all that obey God when he could say know in adverse condition Abraham obey God so we are receiving the promise of the Holy Spirit through faith gelation 3:14. Now I tell the two that always waring the Flesh and the Spirit these are the Flesh which nobody need: idolatry, witchcraft, hatred, variance, emulation, wrath, strife, seditions, gossiping, adultery, fornication, uncleanness, lasciviousness, envy, murders and drunkenness don't do these thing what to need to do every day the fruit of the Spirit: Love, peace, longsuffering, gentleness, goodness, faith, meekness, temperance that what we need to do every day then we will eventually be fill with the Holy Spirit. Galatians 5:16 to 26 we Christian are guided by the thing Jesus need us to do and say to you do it. We trusted in a living savior which we know is alive today and coming back to rule the world Jesus is seal and mark messiah he show the scare of the nail prints in is hand and side that was piece and is feet so that we know is he., we believe are seal with the promise of the Holy Spirit which is earnest of our inheritance until the redemption of the purchase possession unto the praise of his glory. So, we the chosen Apostles, prophets are built upon the foundation being the chief cornerstone., growth unto the Holy temple of the Lord in whom we are built together for a habitation of God through the Spirit Ephesian 2:20 to 22 so make sure our foundation is solid and it should be Jesus unmovable and unshakeable.

2019 I was in Dallas Texas in the US I hear my phone beep off there going to be a tornado coming in my mind I say Lord it a sick joke but that was warning from the weather man and yes, the tornado come and destroy homes some of you would say the foundation was not strong but make our sure foundation is Jesus that can never be move. So, we have to bow to the Father that the whole family of the in heaven and earth is name and Jesus strengthened us by is Spirit make sure our root is ground in the Love of God that only he can give, Early I give the Gift of the Spirit now I am giving 5-fold ministry that we all apart of pick one that you are operate in right now in 2020 some of you for plenty of year congratulation

:Prophets, evangelist, pastors, and teacher is like in the work place owner, manager, supervisor, assistant and worker is the in the global body of Christ worldwide. but it different in doing and must be in the Holy Spirit operation and for the perfecting of the saints for the work of the ministry and for the edifying of the Body of Christ we must operation in these gifts in unity. Try not to grieve the Holy Spirit be holy but make sure we put the armor of God so we are protected properly take the helmet of salvation and the sword of Spirit which is the word of God, praying always in prayer and supplication in the Spirit so we may open our mouth boldly to speak God word read all in Ephesian 6 everyday Christian just put all the armor and the fruit of the spirit every single day. When you see the Police, soldiers and security guard they always have their weapon and always on the alert in case they get an attacked so that how we Christian must be prepare every time. Paul speaks to the colossi church and he encourage them to declare the Spirit in Love and pray that we may be fill with the knowledge of God in all wisdom and spiritual understanding and be fruitful in every good work of the Lord. So, to all my reader I know this is long study on the HOLY SPIRIT but that how important it is that what give you truth and understanding of who God Jesus is so you out there need to know when the kindness and the Love of God appear according to his mercy, he saves us all by the washing of regeneration and renewing of the Holy Spirit, it energizes us big time, and make his Angels Spirit. So, God bearing us with witness both with his sign and wonders and with divers' miracles and the glorious gift of the "HOLY SPIRIT" according to his own will so we see clearly the Holy Spirit is a gift we need to have just like in the natural we receive gift on our wedding day, or birthday the Holy Spirit is most important to have it for life if we take care of it while we have it. When King David sin against God when he was praying forgiveness, he says in is prayer "Jesus take not your Holy Spirit from me" because he knows if the Holy Spirit is gone, he is done like King Saul that hit home to me. So, when you hear the Holy Spirit let him come right in your heart to change you to Jesus for the prophecy came not in old time by the will of man but Holy men of God spoke as they were move and prompted by the Holy Spirit. So, when you keep the commandment, we know that Christ abide in us compliment of the Holy Spirit which he gives us freely Jesus don't charge us nothing he pay for everything so we can have it. Now this is warning try the Spirit if it's of God because many false prophets gone out in this world the sign of the real Jesus is: every Spirit that confess that Jesus Christ come in the flesh is of God, the false Spirit we must watch out for is: If they don't believe Jesus come in flesh there are not of God very important read it 1 John 4:1 to 3 near revelation. Jesus Christ never comes by water only but by water and blood and is the Spirit that near witness because the real Spirit is truth. Every born again need to hear this face the three most important things that bear witness in heaven is: the Father, the Word and Holy Spirit so we see again the Holy Spirit from begin as mention in Genesis 1:2 The three things that bear witness here on earth is: the Spirit again both in heaven and earth, the water and the blood you see in every aspect of God creation the Holy Spirit is so much present. For all those who don't believe on Jesus and just God have surprise coming God say of you don't believe on my son Jesus cannot believe in me God, because Jesus is only to God., 1 John 5:9 to 12.

So, when we have the Holy Spirit, we are different in talking, in action we set apart because that what the Holy Spirit do it transform our whole being in the super human being God nature, so build up yourselves on your most Holy faith I hope you are praying in the Holy Spirit the next big and most important one keep ourself in the Love of God that work hand in hand the Holy Spirit and Love then faith and obeying must we are told to do. The next and finally Apostle I giving is John the dearest lover of the 12 apostle he was in the Spirit when Jesus reveal himself to John in most distinguish and profound way saying "I Jesus am the Alpha and Omega the beginning and the ending saith the Lord to John which is and which was and which is to come the Almighty" Jesus was revealing the last days message to John because of the Spirit John have in him he hears the voice of our soon coming King. Its reminder when I was at my workplace over 25 years when I hear Jesus' voice speaking to me and telling what he needs me to do such a mellow voice tender and loving voice I will never forget that day I can surely say there is on alive savior and his name Jesus. Jesus continue to speak to John saying "I am Alpha and

Omega the first and the last: and what thou sees, write in a book and send to it unto the seven churches which are in Asia unto Ephesus, and unto Smyrna, and unto Pergamos, and unto Thyatira, and unto Sardis, and unto Philadelphia, and unto Laodicea" that Jesus giving John the message to give to the different churches it mean right now as we moving to preach to different ministry we have to seek Jesus for the Holy Spirit word every time you stand to preach don't do in your own intellect but seek Jesus and the Holy Spirit for the word to talk else you will be running a dead ministry with empty benches and no body to preach is not our way is Jesus way. So, we see when John gets this timely prophesy, he was searching to see Jesus but instead he gave 7 candle stick revelation 1:8 and 11 so we see it was different messages for the different church because it was Holy Spirit motivated. So, we see in the different churches only few Gods approve just like lot ministries all over this world but it just few Jesuses name, out of these seven churches is the only the Philadelphia Church was approved here by Jesus that bad because we are not obeying Jesus' way of doing thing. The Pergamos Church was very bad because we have this jezebel woman teaching in the temple and seduce God servant to commit fornication and to eat thing sacrifice unto idol, Jesus tells her about her sin and she repent not the pending judgment for her is revelation 2:20 to 23 and Jesus will kill her children with dead and all believer will know that I search the heart and rein of men so you see when Jesus tells us to stop sin and we don't want them its consequence for our action. When I was writing this book I went to the store and was exchanging out so good for a government card I get here in the US but the worker of the store says it cannot work like that so I warn not to do again else it will be a charge yes that clear warning well we are saying we must stop lie, cheat, gossiping etc. because right now we see this world is upside down big time let Jesus be the center of our life Israel Houghton sing song name " Jesus is the center of our life" it so true. So, John was getting more of Jesus revelation as it unfolds to his knowledge and the Spirit over whelm him here come the throne of God and he see Jesus in is Kingly attire sat on his throne so you see when he was here on earth, he wasn't working for the early throne but the Heavenly one that supersede the earthly one because Jesus Christ will both rule the earthly one and heavenly one because he own it all. I am asking you out there which throne are you working for answer your question?

So, we see in the word of God when you die in Christ we shall raise again because the Spirit in us make it possible but don't let the devil get your soul else you are done that what he is fighting for our soul from day one holds on to Jesus to let him go even when thing is bad still whole on to him never let go. John hears the voice of Jesus say "write blessed are the dead which die in the Lord from henceforth: yea saith the Spirit that they may raise again because of the Spirit that in them revelation 14:12 to 13. Jesus carry John away in the Spirit and saw the mysterious women well dress in expensive clothe having seven head and ten horn she have golden cup it a catch be careful believers, the cup was full of abomination and filthiness of her evil fornication upon her forehead was a name written "MYSTERY BABYLON THE GREAT THE MOTHER OF HARLOTS AND ABOMINATION OF THE EARTH" and John saw the drunken with the blood of the saints and martyrs you have to watch for these jezebel that come to falsify Jesus work don't give in revelation 17:5 the end of the stubborn was Jesus burn her alive she be no more to deceive us, so we rejoice over her out come the apostles, and prophets so we don't have to fight back Jesus fight our battle every day., the secret after she pass in her was found the blood of prophets and of saints and all who she slain on earth.. and the judgement was the devil that deceive the people all over the world was also burn in lake of fire not to be seen or heard no more every evil will come to an end someday. So, the Spirit get greater on John he was in a high mountain to see the real paradise so he sees the gold and diamond of our paradise which we will inherit soon no night no day because God Jesus will be our everlasting live and there will be peace, joy and love unlimited no war and all nation that Jesus chose will be there make sure you live Holy to inherit this true paradise. Hear Jesus word to John saying, "Behold I come quickly blesses is he that kept the saying of the prophesy of this book and behold I Jesus come quickly and my reward is with me to give every man according as his work shall be." Ans John fell at the Angel feet that show all this end time revelation and he worship anywhere you are out there continue words that I am Alpha and Omega the beginning and the end the first and last, I Jesus have sent mine Angel to testify unto you these things in all the churches all over the world I am the root and the offspring of David and the bright and morning star". And the Spirit speak true John so we see in the Word of God name the "Holy Bible "the revelation of this most specially gifts all God Children the Prophets, Pastors, Bishops and member have to use to speak we as now believers can still tarry and get it if we don't have it not too late., the Spirit is communications and passage to God and Jesus if we need correct and truth information about the Kingdom operations. Amen

CHAPTER 8:

PRAYER AND LOVE

"Give ear o lord unto our prayer and attend to the voice of our supplications."- Psalm 86:6

Prayer and love go hand in hand god is love our heavenly father he created us is people and the world in love if you are a true believer we must have the DNA of god love in our heart not sexual love or the fleshy love but the spirit and godly love, apostle Paul write in 1 Corinthians 13 say thou we speak with the tongue of men and of angels and have not love we are nothing it go further thou we prophecy and understand all mysteries and have all knowledge and faith so we move mountain, even if you bestow all you good and feed the poor and give your body to burn, thou we preach and teach god word and have not love we are nothing. god, Jesus, love, faith and obedient with the spirit run the kingdom of God. god created all thing with the root of love and happiness so we can enjoy all he gave us, are you enjoying God creation answer, he gave us family, friends, believers, beaches, places to travel to. I could go on make sure you are enjoying it; I am surely enjoying myself that Jesus gave me he privileges me to travel and see the world for what it is and of course I preach is word to everyone he allows me to and after I do God work, I get my vacation. love must be the source of everything we do in the kingdom of God and in our personal we can enjoy family, enjoy your family in Jesus, enjoy co-worker, enjoy food. don't be use by demonic people don't let them fool you to believe that sex, beating you, abusing you is because I love you I do it okay. watch out for them pray and ask Jesus who to marry, who should be your friends and where to worship it super important only Jesus see the heart of people is recommendation is first, the realtor can tell you anything when you are buying a house because he want to sell, your partner can tell you they love you and is not true because simple they just need some flesh and something you have, your friends can tell you anything because they need something from you, but when you pray to Jesus and seek is approval he speak truth and your life will be very enrich and prosperous and long term happiness and relationship.

Prayer is talking to god like we talk to family, friend is the same rule apply but the difference when you are talking to Jesus we have to repent of all the things we do wrong and surrender to him just like when you going to a lawyer you have to consult them before they work for you and sometime pay them but to talk to Jesus is access free., come in reverent to him not just when we need things like material things or a favor, but come in thanksgiving, come to honor the king come praise is wonderful name come and adore him, sometime when we pray don't ask him for anything just honor him like lord you are good, you are great, you are amazing, you are different from the false god of the world every knee shall bow and every tongue shall confess that you are the only living god. because you pray a heartfelt faith prayer some time God surprise us with what we never ask for like more faith, more love, more of his spirit, more self-esteem, more beauty, more wisdom, knowledge and understanding, money, promotion and opportunity that job and people cannot give to you. I hear of people only have couple dollar left and go play game and won millions of dollar that how god bless us when you serve him in spirit and in truth, Jesus say when you serve me I will bless you and your generation like father Abraham, king David, queen Esther, apostle Moses, Joshua, Gideon and many other god blessing is unlimited no ending to god blessing my reader the bible says seek he first the kingdom of god and all is righteousness and all things will be added multiply unto you, that why as god sold out children we are wonderfully bless. this book god gave me to write I know it is here to stay for a long time because Jesus gives me the idea to write this timely book. I tell what prayer I do was inspire and motivated because I was in couple days praying and fasting when Jesus says get a pen and paper and start write and I did but the devil also never let it happen I put down the manuscript give the publisher some and never give them all they call but I never response. but Jesus appears back to me and say start write back this book and I did, I glad I did because I know for sure soul will be save, deliver, bless, heal and prosper true this best seller from the highest god. make prayer, praise, reading god word be our lifestyle get an addiction to god so miracle can happen without you even let a pastor touch or preach to you get this relation with Jesus at the highest level a man in the bible name Enock was spirit fill they never tell about his position whether he is a priest or prophet the bible say he was translated to god alive because of the spirit and faith in god the word of god say some will be alive when Jesus come they will never taste of dead that the truth. Apostle Moses and Aaron pray to free the Israelites From bondage and Moses pray every step of the way until they were totally free when they came to this country god engage Moses in prayer 40 days and 40 night and let Moses write the commandment in exodus 20 Moses was in prayer and the spirit motivation when you are in the present of the lord that how you are fill to preach and pray and do the things of god just like some people when they take drug or smoke they do crazy thing because the drug influence them let the spirit influence you and not wrong things. until present we now generation have to abide by the commandment because of prayer, when they sin against God Moses have to pray for God wrath to stay so they never get destroy. In January of 2022 when I was writing this book I hear my phone beep loud when I look they say it going to be a tornado in my area I start to pray Jesus please move away the tornado just a simple prayer for help it was like I was praying for a hour it just what I tell you, I am happy to report my caring Jesus let the tornado hit somewhere else, I was sick on many occasion and I pray the healing prayer say *Jesus send his word and heal us in Psalm 107:20*, you was wounded for my transgression you are bruise for our inequity the chastened of your peace was upon us and by you stripe we are heal* I get my healing my deliverance because of faith believing prayer so all my reader when you pray believe and have faith and expecting that it will happen just like you work you are expecting to get pay don't it? Don't rush to read the bible and good book like these because you need to get the sense of what you read and apply it to your life okay you don't understanding what you are reading stop and pray and say Jesus what this book mean or the bible, some time when I am reading the bible or good book I stop and say Jesus what that mean I never read until it know what it mean, some time is not the dictionary will give you the meaning is the holy spirit job okay prophetic word from god.

This house I am living right now I move in without asking permission because I apply Jesus' word, he says I give you house you never work for; I give you money you never work for and again he says occupied until I come I do it more than one time and it work. I remember when I was in Boston Massachusetts preaching, they take my jacket it was cold I take a jacket in the store and bring to the cashier without no money the cashier cash it where is the money little after a young Man Came to The Cashier and I ask him to buy it yes, he purchases the jacket for me that faith, the young man say I don't have it because I have my children to take care of but on second thought he pay for it. Have faith in God people always ask apostle Claudia, how you travel around the world preaching and you don't work I tell them, and I am telling you let God faith work and pay all your bill put faith in action. For example, you don't have gas money, but you drive your car or go at the bus stop without money because you know for sure god will send someone to buy you gas and give you bus fare and of course they did; tell God thank, that call for relationship with Jesus everyday so you can know your benefits in him not in religion but a personal relationship with the master Jesus. Just like you marry you husband you become one because of the marriage so you are automatically entitled to what he has because you are wife, that when you serve Jesus and obey is commandment you automatically become children of God, he put us first you must know the right in God by praying and reading his word just like a will that left for you if you don't read the will, you can't know don't it.

The love that bears our trial in a relationship god love will be tested in all way for instance you lose your job, you are sick, etc. Are you going to leave your husband or wife I hope not, I was reading an article on the couple that the wife was burn severally she become unattractive I saw the picture of her but the husband still love her, he say I never marry for just good look I marry a good heart women, how much husband would do what this true lover do that god love in that man the original wedding vow say *for better or for worst for richer or poorer is you partner* love who god gave us just like that young man. God is the headquarter of love he created loved and we are the recipient and beneficiary of god love every day in my prayer I say Jesus I love you I need all that love in me I want to be the rose garden and carry of you love and presence so far so good, I got the love of my heavenly father big time lot for even the enemy this love you have to pray for everyday not sexual love but the love that you smile, share and give and love who you see every day. The greatest commandment is *love the lord with all your heart, mind and soul and love your neighbors as yourself this message we hear from the beginning.* Martin Luther king say *love is the most powerful weapon in the university* late Abraham Lincoln was bold to free us slave because he love all people* Jesus our lord and savior Jesus was bold to give is life on the cross because of the great love*, one of Jesus disciple john was a lover of the 12 apostle that Jesus say when he was leaving earth *john take care of my mother* he could ask the other 11 but they never have that great love like john. Love is not positive or title or money, but you love the person heart and that person must love you back. When I think about my biological father name Nathan palmer when he was alive I saw him give, help in manner that only few people do he would bring food to people, get job for them, have party for the whole neighborhood I hear him always say to my mother when you cook leave some because somebody may be hungry, that love in action he is with the lord now at much safer place and at rest., by the way my biological father never molest me or nobody he was just a good man that have a good heart, because some people tend to get touchy. We must pray for god and spirit to give us new way of giving, loving and communicate I let the spirit lead me some time I go preaching, sometime I go feed the poor and fellowship just be friendly with the people but before I go I pray say Jesus let it be joyous, let the people enjoy my presentation you want the people to enjoy what you give to them including preaching god word some preacher or so boring and dry in their presentation that why can safely say get the spirit pray for elders, choir leader and people to sing, musician, prayer warrior, missionary, young people ministry, you see the apostle Paul appoint and ordain elders and ministry as he travel to the different places and Jesus how he appoint his disciples he pray to god before they was appointed judas fail because of money like some of us let the devil tempt you with material things and flesh and you lose out on God but you can come back repent and come back not too late., peter let down Jesus when he need help but peter repent and come back to god and he make him head of the 11 apostle, even king David sin against god and David repent and come back to Jesus yes a man after god own heart so I am calling all the backslider come home to Jesus he is waiting for you there is room for you like the prodigal son in the bible he take his passion from his father and leave and get broke but he return back home when his father saw him coming back home he give him a welcome party big word again *forgiveness* go and forgive who hurt you all my reader. I see the story on television the man kills the women daughter and go to jail and come out but the mother forgives him and not only that they are good friend oh yes right here in America. When Jesus was on the cross the same people that kill, he says father forgive them because they don't know what they have done great forgiveness, when they stone steven before he dies, he says father don't charge it against them praise God get a relationship It easy when you are in a relationship with Jesus.

For Jesus to have a famous and successful ministry he have to fast and pray that anywhere he preach people get save, delivery, heal and dead body heal the spirit and prayer that take the world like world wind of course that great love was present with him, he lay down the model prayer in Matthew 6:9 let I interpret this prayer to you all after this manner we pray *our father which art in heaven hallowed be they name meaning before you pray honor god, thy kingdom come thy will be done on earth as it is heaven meaning is kingdom is preach in word and do is work here on earth like give and help, give us this day our daily bread meaning he provide personal need like money, housing etc., forgive us our debts as we forgive our debtors meaning forgive who hurt you, lead us not into temptation but deliver us from evil for thine is the kingdom the power and the glory for every amen meaning avoid sin and evil says no to doing evil. That the interpretation of this well know prayer you don't have to pray the exactly prayer but it the rule of this prayer the spirit will tell how to pray okay pray in God will. Bad prayer that done get answer from Jesus some of us pray to hurt people and be seen and we don't repent before we pray, Jesus will not answer your prayer when we don't repent of our sin, go at a quiet place and pray and pray for all your enemies too those prayer get God attention forgive them. When Jesus was here on earth and was praying all is, prayer was answer because it prays from a clean heart and right spirit, that spark power and freedom and liberty. We must want to be like Jesus let him be our inspiration our hero Jesus is my hero, Whitney Houston, Michael Jackson, Denis brown, Bob Marley and Luther Vandross, these people are the love angels of the world of that until present their music and inspiration is be listen and watch by this now generation I know for sure this book will pass on to all generation name *my mess become our message of love* letting people know we don't have to be bitter because we have a bad pass like me and other I personally chose to let go and let god and forgive who hurt us, including family, friend and Christians the bible said leave all revenge unto me I will repay sons and daughter so don't retaliate. Jesus was beaten bloody but he never retaliate he take the punches for me and you so we may live and be free so do the same in the kingdom of god we have to make sacrifice for god and ourself, sometime pray and fast no physical food do something that not normal but let Jesus and the spirit lead you, what good for me is not what good for you everybody is different and unique different fingerprint even if we are twins that how different we are, a pastor was telling me about an orphanage in Africa that the children get burn by fire at the time when she tell me I feel I was being push, I say to her let I pray because I like to be led not push, I love children I always have my children charity going if you want to bless this ministry and my charity let me know you can call 754 368 9454 when I pray I just know god says help the children because I was led not push the same week I send money to different ministry in Africa and ministry here in America I am cheerful giver but led to give not push they say where you heart is that where you treasure is that where you must help.

Let stay in the family of god not going with people that don't believe in our god and our values it will call separation sooner or later, David son Solomon that god chose to take over from David which god love he told Solomon don't take these women because they will lead you to worship there false god and turn your heart from me, and Solomon disobey god and go with these Pegan women and build temple to house there false god and god was upset with Solomon that really going too far in sin he sleep with them but he take it further he use god money and build expensive temple for them. God take the throne from him he loss because of disobedient, that what happen when you make bad choice, and samson the same way he marry strange women and the women let him die we talking don't be with unequally yoke it will cost you your life, your jobs, your salvation, your character and your marriage, I met a man couple here in Florida telling me he and his wife marry for over 2 year when he gone to work she empty is bank account and take most of the furniture and gone yes is wife he taught she love him but she love his money not the man that making bad choice lady you bad watch out for these evil people. Making right choice: now *father Abraham want a wife for his son Isaac he tells his son don't take none of these women in the land that we live but I sent my servant to my people to get you a wife that a good father because as a man of God he sees the future ahead and they bring him back a wife for is son and of course that marriage last because of right choice and father Abraham and his wife Sarah last until they die. I next good choice I see my own mother and father marry and live for many years until my father pass of course they have their moment but they never break up it was loving my mother was so jealous because my father is a very understanding lover even to our community. I met a guy not even couple days all he talk about is flesh right away I tell him stay far I never off to pray to god and ask him if this young man is my husband right there because of his conversation I know he is not my type, relationship don't base on sex and money else it will surely fail okay he even offer me money I tell him know I don't want his money don't let satanic people buy you with money, last summer of 2021 they text me offer me millions of dollar for fame and serving the devil readily I say know nothing shall separate me from my Jesus no money, no sex, no fame absolutely nothing my relationship teach me depend on god for everything including personal things so much disease going around after they give you the money they leave disease on you that money cannot care take heed all my reader we love you all and do not want to see the devil destroy you and your family wait on god if I can say no to the devil you can too I am a regularly women just like anyone out there but I choose Jesus and his peace and just addicted to do good thing that all my choice is Jesus all the way let Jesus be your choice amen. That why it most important to seek God for your partner and not just flesh and material things. we see family love how Jacob love his son joseph out of all his children and David love Solomon out of all his children they were impartial those children turn out to be love by god too, I see growing up it was 6 children my mother have but my father turn out to love me more and guess what, Jesus love me too that he chose to use me to bring is good new to the world so all along my father was right about me, so far I travel to England, Canada, all over the USA California, new Hampshire, Boston, new York, new jersey, Delaware, Maryland, north and south Carolina, Georgia, Texas, new Arlene and all over the USA and my home state Florida everywhere I travel to my resting place and vacation place is south Florida and Jamaica I am so comfortable le and at peace., which I think is the best state. right now, planning to travel to Canada to preach and help so many people Jesus is calling to do something in the kingdom of God but you don't want to do it, I come to tell you obey God and do it he will give you all the resource you need he provide all I need plane ticket, housing, food, gas for my car and all I need he will do the same for you make sure you have relationship with Jesus. couple year right here in Florida I was out doing mission I saw this young lady in the rain on the road with her sign witnessing in the pouring rain that the love of god in action, so you can hear from him direct or where you worship make sure the pastor connect to god the bible say go where my name is so everything will be easy for all we need to know when we go out and witness and the people come to Jesus they can stay where god put them, just like you marry but the husband treat you bad he beat you, treat you like slave and don't help you I know you not going to stay. Sometime people would complain to me say sister Claudia I was going at such and such ministry but they hurt me I have to left there really, when I check it out sometime it true because I have similar experience with Christian and pastor so again pray to god where to go worship it such ashamed to see you go at temple that should be safe and holy and it turn out to be a war zone, faith is the big word in the kingdom of god utilize your god given faith move forward sound advice pray to Jesus and ask him where to worship especially in these last days we need holy spirit word, we need to grow mature in god and been fed with the word of god so we can be ready when Jesus come, Jesus say wo to them that lead my sheep astray that a warning form the messiah.

I am sorry to say some preacher is just not connected to God when you read the bible it warns you of false prophets and false preacher but when you have the spirit of truth in you it will reveal to you, I am not casting a stone or putting no one under condemnation is just the truth, the prophet Jeremiah warn a lot about false preacher and prophets and priest read the book of Jeremiah. when you read the bible, you see the true church let go St. mark 16:17 very important word from the apostle mark * these sign shall follow them that believe in my Jesus' name we shall cast out devil, they shall speak with new tongue, they shall take up serpent and if they drink any deadly things, it shall not hurt them, we shall lay hand on the sick and they shall recover* are you seeing these things happening where you worship? Jesus pay is life for this church so it very important to him and our father god so we cannot falsified the church and do what it right in our own eyes, we have to follow what Jesus need and want not what we want okay so we as god children have to defend god holiness and peace I very good at defending what Jesus stand for because I get save the right and proper way I never get religion I get Jesus in my heart mind and soul, that why when I get the offer from the devil agent I never think twice I turn it down that the difference just like how you fight for your family, friend, country apply the same rule fight for Jesus defend him don't defend title and position okay. I see recently the devil targeting the church 2021 pastor killing member, member shot and kill in the house of God, little 6-year-old rape in the house of God going to the rest room some of these pastors supposed to be preaching God word they are using curse word the spirit of truth tells you those word not of

God I could go on. In the early church back there in Israel there was a pastor and his wife was pastoring the church but because of envy they commit murder yes the pastor and his wife there is man in the same place he have a vineyard we call it rose garden the pastor and his wife covet the man vineyard and conspire with the people of Israel and go on prayer and fasting and kill the man so we see some prayer pray is not of god, because before they kill the man they pray and fast get this in your spirit but god step in and both of them that kill the man die most disgracefully god himself take revenge that the early church, and one more evil that done in the early church so you see what going on in these temple it use to happen the apostle go to the church and one of the church sister treat them so bad curse them out but these early preacher never reply back so these evil start in the church a long time but it don't have to continue. Solution we have to start pray connecting and faith fill prayer and bring back respect and sincerity with holiness to the church so people will want to come and stay we have to bring back peace to the house of God else people will not come and stop come. Our job as apostle and prophets and evangelist and who care to share God word you don't have to preach to share God word if the word is in your heart go ahead and share it, so go where they are bang on those doors, preach in the train and bus where they are in the prison and work place anywhere on earth, they are we have to reach them and bring them in the house of God. Just like you have a family member missing or friend you go look for them don't it, so we don't want when they come, they have to leave and don't come back okay. let search our heart and pray for Jesus and his blood to clean us up and start live for the one that go the extra mile for us *Jesus* the real super star do it for Jesus, anywhere we go people must see Jesus in us the gentleness, the love, peace and joy even before we talk our presence must reflect whom we are in god.

Love and prayer combine learning the god way he says my wisdom is not of this world its foolishness to the fleshy knowledge, but my wisdom, knowledge and understanding come from me God and it spiritual learn true the spirit. King Solomon was the most sought after teaching he says * by the spirit of the lord a wise man will hear and will increase learning and a man of understanding shall attain unto wise counsels, the fear of the lord is the beginning of knowledge turn you at my reproof behold I god will pour out my spirit unto you all I will make known my words unto you the back drop of god word and knowledge is the spirit, so have the spirit have love and pray to get the word that will be powerful. When you do it God way, you will be safe, successful, prosperous and never be defeated when I was in the state of Georgia last November 2021, I clearly hear Jesus loudly says *daughter the devil is defeated* don't worry we have the victory true Christ Jesus so keep this victory alive we are saved, we are grateful, we are cover by the blood that some of what give us God victory amen. David victory talk says *there shall no plaque come near our dwelling because he gives is precious angel charge over us to keep us safe, a next assurance he gives us hold on to is unchanging hand he will never leave us nor forsake us.

Prayer for direction and choice: the leader Jesus was about to choose is disciple but what he do before he chose, he pray to god to show him who to choose in Luke 6:12 and 13 Jesus pray all night and pick up all his apostle at work and where he would be we are children of god he that know and serve Jesus hear us he that is not of god hear us not, is sheep hear his voice he say I came for the lost sheep of my house so he came for those who gone astray. Beloved let love one another for indeed love is of God everyone that have love is of God. That the attachment typing this manuscript there is time when I am saving my writing the computer say merge to the next file it a message of God let us merge to our brother and sister because we have the same spirit in us. when we merge together as one Jesus change our name to holiness and unity like the 11 apostles in unity and one accord to receive the holy spirit. do you want to call Holiness Children of God? I know you want to call that name because we are children of god he put us first before anyone, many prophets and pastor want to see what we see and hear and cant because they are not of our tribe, secret belong to us I read a book that this sister write she say she see Jesus and Jesus Was Preaching to her that god children, I see Jesus speaking to me on many occasion and see the man in person because I am a child of go one of the message I clearly remember it was about love plain as day I enjoy it be in the spirit of god to see these awesome thing of god and he always show movie when I first got save in Jamaica beautiful, spectacle that the truth I get a glimpse of god paradise I am so honor be encourage my brother and sister if you leave mother, father, house and land and come home to Jesus he will restore us you will receive greater manifold in the future world to come restoration is you. Make Jesus temple a holy house of prayer and reverence respect the house respect your body because it the church of the living god, all things must be fulfilled which was spoken by the prophets concerning me Jesus' repentance and remission of sins to all people around the world. Love assurance the king says to Solomon because the lord loves his people, he makes us kings and queen over all people.

Prayer of protection by the priest Ezra 8:21 he proclaims a fast there at the river of ahava so our journey is safe from the enemies our families is safe because I never want to use the band of soldiers Jesus protect us from all evil: so, our weapon was prayer and fasting to God to clear the way for safe travel, so if these early Christian can pray for everything including protection, we present Christian must follow these example and pray to put away all gun, knife and all deadly weapon. God deliver them from the hand of the enemies they reach their destination safely because they pray and fast. When I personally have a problem the first thing I do is pray and ask God to help me that what relationship tell you to do so start having a relationship with God big time. Nehemiah was chosen of God to rebuilt the wall but before he builds the wall, he prays o lord, I beseech thee let now thine ear be attentive to the prayer of your servant who desire to fear they name and prosper we pray thee thy servant this day grant us mercy in the sight of these people I am the king cupbearer. are we praying and seeking God like these chosen man and women of God? How to pray we pray through the holy spirit with Jesus leading all prayer and most importantly with a repentative heart. There is book I read that one of the best prayer book I ever read name *how to pray* by author Ronnie Floyd every Christian especially prayer warrior should read this prayer book I read this book 3 time it lead us to god answering our prayer with the best book on planet earth the *holy bible* read it is when I start get serious with Jesus and start get in prayer and reading the word with the holy spirit I start get the word big time, it like watching a movie when I am reading the bible that how the spirit let it appear. That you can't get boring reading the bible because the power of the holy spirit juice it up so it sweet like some orange juice and sweet wine.

My though: faith and prayer, love and peace are the vitamins of the soul no human being can live without God nitrous vitamins, so take you medicine every day from Jesus' medicine cabinet. I was in houston Texas 2019 preaching God word and realize when I leave houston I loss some of my memory I pray to Jesus to restore my memory, I could not wait I see the ads on YouTube about tablet for memory lost and sent and get some when I take the tablet all it does open my appetite, I have to stop take them right now as I write this book it improving every day without me taking these tablets. Believe in every detail of what Jesus word says and what Jesus the person say act in faith and you will be restore like all the miracle we read in the bible, believe my friends and you shall receive and expect it to come like your expecting to get your children to come from school please take care of your children and be protected of other children that not your own they are the one that going to take our place a love children and pray that they put back prayer in the school here in America and anywhere it missing we can't afford no more war in the school.

The chosen queen Esther that prays her way to the top of God throne and won all her battle we can do the same, pray stop complain and fight, the queen in the bible she was coming from jail when she and her uncle decide to go to a different country never know what would have happen, like all of us when we are cast down, push aside, loss everything, rejecting we tense to try something than not doing anything well Esther do just that. When she came to this strange country, she was just in time for the beauty pageant that was about to take place you see God position Esther and her uncle for blessing favor and promotion she never knows what god was up to but God know she was the women for the job. watch this some of us ladies would not have enter because of where we coming from our self-esteem is crush don't it: but this courageous women got the courage to enter this prestigious competition and she won all the other contestant, god work continue in her when she realize there was a wicked man want to kill all her people call the jews and her uncle send and tell queen Esther about the plot that should have carry out, look what Esther do he call his uncle and tell him go tell all my people we going on 3 days prayer and fasting to destroy the plans of the enemies, now Esther never say let pick up our weapon and we fighting back but she resort to prayer and fasting that why god chose her in the first place because he was looking on heart and a character that would bring out is instruction. After the 3 days prayer and fasting god destroy all the enemies that want to kill Esther people and their families what a victory the song say *victor is our victory today in 2022 and beyond his our* receive your victory dance and shout thank you Jesus get a praise break put down the book a little while and praise Jesus for your victory are you fighting a battle probable sickness, stress, insecurities, family problems, poverty or enemies like Esther apply Jesus pray and let god fix it for you he will take care of everything you give him to do but make she you give Jesus and not the witches or the satanic people god children get your crown and wear your spiritual crown of joy, peace, love and holiness when you have that first in your heart then go to the store and buy your crown and wear it to complete your victory do it, instruction from Jesus this is an action book not just read but act on it.

Chose who this day you will serve we can't serve two God is just one true god we must serve is name is Jesus the son of the living god he is our mediator between man and God, hold on to his unchanging hand never let him go. This song goes like this *draw me close to you never let me go* next song say *nearer my god to thee nearer to thee* in all life challenges we go through never give up on God he will never give up on us. I personally see God work in my life when all is gone family, friends and Christians I learn to trust God, he never fails us yet, I see it should have die, in jail I was suicidal, have low self-esteem but thank to Jesus in my darkness time here come Jesus to hold my hand and heart and rest assure he will do the same for you all. Your loneliness will not be forever, your sickness will not be forever, your poor situation will not be forever. This single mother right here in the USA no father in the house only she alone take care of her children in 2021 the president was giving out money because of the covid virus a lot of people could not work, guess what the special single mother get her money and you would think she would buy food for her children and clothes, but she invest the money in coaching business never know like queen Esther that it would make a turnaround, it never take long for the money she invest make her a fortune of millions of dollar. My lord it not the little you have like this single mother but how you can turn it around little is much when you can use or spent wisely. Jesus was healing people back those days doing all the miracle for over three day the people stick with Jesus for three days never eat nothing because they need their miracle after the three days there were angry, guess what Jesus do there was a little boy with just few fishes and little bread but they bring it to Jesus and he bless it and feed over five thousand people it shares because of who bless it the master Jesus. Right now if you believe and expect whether little or a lot it will happen for you it happen for Oprah, it happen for Denise brown and bob Marley, it happen for serena and Venus William, it happen for Michael Jackson and Whitney Houston, Jeff Bezos he was in an orphanage when someone adopt him and know he is one of the richest man in the world the good thing he build a homeless shelter for the homeless, Tyler perry was homeless when god bless him it, Mike Tyson was on the street when god bless him to be a champion, and Kevin hart the long list go on it will happen for you. These name it give you these people coming from a very poor background, but they perceive and use their god given talent and it was very successful. so, use what god gave you a talent, a craft, a trade, an education etc. Use it up and bless Jesus, yourself and other don't hide the gift god gave you my brother and sisters, stop going around envying people and fight against people you can do.

When Christ live in our heart our nature change, our personality change, love evolve in our nature and our very image of who we are transform., change start with us if we really want to change answer do you want to change?...put in your name if you mean you want to change, we are living in world don't let people change you are your environment change you be like Jesus he was in the world like us born and grow like us 100% man and 100% god and he never let nothing change who he is, if you are in friendship and people want to change you to somebody you not approve of tell them know and leave there friendship as it say early in this book pray for friends and who to be with because later you will be sorry you marry the wrong person, sorry you stick with that friends that leading you astray to give in to peer pressure my friends it personal have to tell some people we can't communicate anymore because they are pulling me back and it have to let them go because where Jesus is taking us it not everyone he will allow to come with you because they will never suffer for Jesus, they will never make sacrifice for Jesus they will not serve him so you cannot be around these people some of the people have negative vibes. I read a book a preacher write he say when God call him, he has to witness to his friend let them know he can't be a part of them anymore because of their negative vibe that a serious man of God, how serious you are with Jesus?...No more or else you will suffer because of your decision you make, so make up your mind what you going to do in 2022 and beyond. I make up my mind it is going forward with Jesus all the way everyday good time and bad time is Jesus he never gives up on us he takes the pain and the shame for us all, he goes the extra mile for the whole world they beat him, they spite on him like a criminal, they give him heavy cross to carry over 82 miles just to redeem us to God for the great love he has for us. World it give you Jesus let him take full control of your heart mind and soul he want to live in you not on a building but he need your heart, mind and soul, just say Jesus save me i am sinner need a savior and the only savior can save you is Jesus no other savior in the world cannot save your soul but Jesus the omnipotent Jesus is power is unlimited he can do anything, omniscient Jesus he have complete knowledge and omnipresent Jesus he is here there and everywhere at the same time. Let Jesus be your teacher, your king of king and lord of lord, our high priest, our sustainer, our protector and guide, let Jesus be you director and father. All I tell you believe and welcome this Jesus in your heart, if you don't invite someone in your home when they knock you will never open the door because you never invite them don't it? For Jesus to work for you and your family invite him in your heart make room for Jesus by praying, let your heart be clean with love, peace and joy, holiness and just say welcome Jesus, welcome sweet holy spirit and welcome great god always says the welcome and thank you Jesus, use these words to him every day not just to people but to the creator that made us.

Declaration: to the highest god and his sons Jesus declare him with other tell people about his amazing good work, and who he really is, this is the love power Jesus that lightening up the whole world with is presence, is awesome creation the heaven and the earth, the rain, the sunshine, the birds, the seas and all that he created he mention in genesis god say everything he created was so good and wonderful. The prophet Isaiah declare Jesus say I saw the lord high and living up and his trail fill the temple, apostle Moses declare god say I saw the lord face to face and he was glorious; I personally saw the lord and he was great, slender, immaculate, royal, loving and peaceful yes I Claudia Henderson see the risen Jesus in person so many times because of the spirit in me my mind blow so many time knowing that I see the risen lord, it a mind blowing experience that only few can see these spectacle thing and I am still living to tell the glory I saw and you can see it to if you have the spirit of god in you, the real spirit of god not the false spirit. Look how peter declare Jesus he was one of Jesus chief disciple he come as living stone disallow indeed of men reject of man but chosen of our father god precious living stone build up on spiritual house a holy priest hood to offer spiritual sacrifice acceptable to God. I don't care who reject you or abandon you and gossiping you they do Jesus the same way, they treat me too, but if God is for you no one dare come against you, God say every knee shall bow and every tongue shall confess that Jesus is lord we are declaring who he is yes, the chapter talking about love and prayer but we have to declare who give us the benefits of prayer, love, faith, the spirit celebrates him honor him and declare him too other. When I was writing this manuscript I stop and was watching YouTube and it so happen I see Dionne Warwick, Aretha Franklyn and Glady knight singing in concert way back when one of the song they were singing was *love in the spirit* I was amaze to see these well-known celebrates sing song that glorified god on big and massive stage with millions of people watching all over the world, my dear friend Whitney Houston always singing gospel song to glorified god song like *Jesus love us this I know* these are well known gospel song in deed there background is from the church that telling me there are not ashamed to talk and sing about Jesus on any stage. Well, are you using your mouth to tell people about Jesus or sing to them about Jesus or even putting up sign that tell people about Jesus, create way to evangelize preach on the bus, the train, the plane, in the mall or shopping center or at work even in your community your neighbor we declaring Jesus not with shut mouth but with action? The prophet Jeremiah declares God to backslidden Israel he was prophet god call from teenage year that when Jeremiah hears the voice of God, Jeremiah reply god, I am little boy I can" t even talks properly but God reply back to Jeremiah open wide your mouth and I God will fill it with words. I say to all my reader open wide your mouth like Jeremiah God will fill it with word you don't have to go to any well-known bible school, Jesus and the spirit will tell you what to say and how to say it, be reliable on Jesus and the spirit ask them to tell us what to say. When I am going to preach, I start by saying Jesus please give me a word, and I say holy spirit fill my mouth with a word for your people because I know that I cannot speak until it from God and the holy spirit. When Jesus was declaring God to enemies, he says all I do I cannot do by myself its God my father in me coming to you that relying on God and not on your own intellect that will fail. When the blind man was heal Jesus heal him for 38 year he was blind but when Jesus heal him he start declaring Jesus to everyone he see because he can see know open wide your mouth and declare god and his son Jesus be not ashamed, the apostle say I am not ashamed of the gospel of Jesus Christ because it freedom and liberty it the power of god unto salvation, Jesus raise Lazarus from the dead and his families and friend start declaring Jesus to every one and all those who was presents seeing the miracle and start believing and declaring Jesus to other when the women that have that blood condition for many year when she meet Jesus she was completely heal she declare Jesus to everyone. Declaration is good you're not preaching but you are declaring who our heavenly father is boast on Jesus amen.

Back to the main topic prayer and love god knows we need some time out to declare who our God is, the prayer of the prophet Habakkuk when Israel sin against God they were stiff necked people every opportunity they get they sin against God so continually God have to raise up different prophet to preach to them even know in this present world Jesus still raising up different preacher and prophet to preach and warn of the ending of the world including me. I take a little of the prophet Habakkuk prayer says *lord I hear thy speech and was afraid lord revive thy work in the midst of the year have mercy on us God came from Taman and the holy one from mount Parana his glory covers the heaven and the earth was full of his praise. So then prophet Habakkuk in his prayer hear the voice of god but he was afraid begging to restore his work and have mercy, we all pray that kind of prayer sometime especially when thing are going down we need restoration in our everyday live we want to be Christlike, we want perfection, we need prosperity nothing wrong with that because god is a prosperity just like people say pastor Credlo dollar always preaching prosperity message nothing wrong with that nobody want to be poor and homeless hear what god say on prosperity through apostle john listen: god in 3 john he states I wish about all thing that all will proper and being in good health even as our soul prosper, he never create us to suffer and live from pay cheque to pay cheque no, he want us to live the abundant life he already provide for us all we need to access it by faith and stop doubting god ability. Pray bold prayer, go get prayer, powerful prayer and believe you shall receive. When I pray, I am expecting Jesus to move on my behave and all those who I pray for. Be optimistic about what God have for all of you surround yourself with holy spirit godly people that can help you like Paul mentor timothy and Titus they were Paul spiritual sons that the apostle Paul leave them to shepherd the churches, before he grooms them before to take it over, God groom is son Jesus before he could fully start his ministry at 30-year-old. Prayer is the root and foundation of all Jesus ministry and love with the icing on the ministry the *holy spirit* that let the power flows, praying without the holy spirit is dead because is the spirit pray and give us the word. More prayer more power no praying no power. Before Jesus suffering he pray he bring peter, James and john with him and they were sleeping when Jesus was praying Jesus says to them could you watch with me, but there flesh give way like some of us that why we have to pray off the flesh from interrupting the spirit it a war from day one the flesh always waring with the spirit keep fighting off the flesh by saying: no sex until I am married, no lying, no war, no unforgiveness, no cheating that fighting of the flesh:, welcoming the spirit is love, peace, joy, obey, live holy, forgive who hurt, be friendly and serve Jesus you are entraining the spirit of god because you need it to live in you and do the work in you.

So love continue to defeat the devil when you act god love by talking to your enemies, ignore negativity, be friendly, be real, stay in the presence of god, keep focus I admire Jesus focus he was just like us grow like us by now you read in the bible Jesus was born in a stable that how low he was but he keep his eye on the one who send him father god and never sin, never get involve in gang and peer pressure it was known or yes for him. His love was perfectly demonstrating in his action I have to pray for focus every day because so many things can cause distraction if you let it sometime is the news, your family, your friends just want to involve in everything that can cause distraction. Time for everything but don't get off track that you lose sight of your purpose and goal you set time management is very important to our focus just say I have to do god work first then everything come after priority is all god want to see in our doing pray first, read the bible first, Jesus say go witness or preach do that first, god say go help the poor today do it first even if something you plan spoil just have an attitude I prefer put Jesus first. When peter and some of the disciple go witness some place, they go they were beaten, rejected and scorn because of Jesus the apostle was beaten and left to dead just because he was preaching God word, but they were happy to suffer for Jesus' sake. I remember when I was in boson state, I was preaching on a bus even some place I preach they curse us, they rob us but my focus is God work have to complete and I finish it. The last word Jesus say *its finish man redemption have been paying* Jesus keeps his focus and finish god assignment gracefully it was pain and suffering but he finishes it. I was bless to be for the first time at the boson marathon but I notice that some of the runner never finish the 26 miles but some finish the race hopping, walking even stopping and rolling but the bottom line they cross the finish line, most important finish what Jesus start in you he still speak son and daughter I so proud of you because you finish all my work I give you to do., I personally know when Jesus gave me this idea to write this book nearly 2 year I was stopping and starting but in 2022 I know that I pick it up back and start again and finish so you can read it and give it to your family and friends pick up what god gave you to do let it be happening now, not later. I see my neighbor was healthy never sick she was going to work looking really good the Sunday we spoke, and I even invite her to the house of God she says next week sister Claudia, guess what couple days her daughter gave me the bad news my mother passes she never sick yet she is not with us anymore, so make sure you finish what is set before you say God.

<u>We declare Jesus we are honoring God</u>: say among all you bless eye on God is great even in your private time with Jesus you create everything perfectly, your love and presence is glorious precious, your provision and protection is like nobody can do, you are magnificent, you are Jehovah shalom meaning peace and unity, you are our whole life, you are our joy, lord you reign the world is established because of you. Every day before I go in prayer I make sure honor god before I start my prayer and worship him before you pray, when you read the bible all the early Christian sing and worship before they preach and pray look the coming of the lord first the bible say it the sound of trumpet first we going to hear, when the children of Israel was in bondage they worship and cry before they get out when they get out they continue to worship god and honor him, king David was a worshipper the greatest worshiper that all the other kings even when king Saul was in trouble with the evil spirit it was David praise and instrument playing heal Saul and king that know to worship the true and living god. Make a joyful noise on to the lord all he people for the lord is high above all the earth god is exalted above all other make is honor glorious. I hear that some churches don't worship and play music if it true it not of god, he have angel 24 hour a day 7 days a week just to worship he god, I was in a dream when I was on prayer and fasting couple year I personnel I love music and the angel come for me I see camera all over me and they bring me in a big house I see a band of angels playing music, and worshipping god it was something to behold I was where the praise made thank Jesus it a honor we are true children of god so we will see, and one time I see the angel they take me into a sea of water paradise I could go on and one but I will write them in my next book. The devil lucifer was the head of the music department in heaven he can sing but when he see god that created him and everyone get the honor and the worship he start getting jealous and envious of the living god, he

start fight and rebel against god and is throne but the warrior angel Michael and Gabriel and the other angel fight him and his gang and put them back down here on earth even some of the falling angels that come with him are in chain until know the second coming of our lord and savior Jesus Christ. So, all god children one of our duties it to honor the living god true worship, praise, be holy let the relationship with Jesus become super easy for you nobody have to push us to read the bible and pray, nobody have to push us to go to the house of God because our relationship with God is our only push you don't have to wait until you go in the temple to access God it every day all day. Just like you married you know you duty as wife and husband tell your spouse every day I love you darling without an anniversary or birthday party that love must be in your heart everyday pray holy spirit to give us new ways of loving our family and friends surprise them sometime with a card, flower a present new clothes, take them out for fellowship or vacation without any specially occasions that the great love we need from Jesus not flesh lusting love that only center on flesh that evil love will fail sooner or later. Be excellent winner for Jesus when last year it was the Olympic where people compete to win different race like track and field, swimming, relay, basketball, baseball and the different sport when I see the winner that win the medals, I say that God they win but I say Jesus I pray they win in the heart, mind and soul in the spirit just like in physical races. I know this basket player he was real Christian when the reporter interview him by my surprise he never have sex he say my Jesus would want me to wait until I am married even in is regular interview he boast about god and he was one of the most successful player in the professional league he say Jesus let him win most of his game by now he is married but bottom line he wait on god, he was wealthy travel the whole world could get any women he need but he wait tell god give him a wife do the same, don't let your ego get a head of you and then you sorry., honoring god mean to wait tell your carouse moment arrive don't get jealous because your friends do thing and you simple can't wait the backlash it never work out for you simple because it was not for you. God have something for each and every one when you pray, honor him and wait until your time come you see somebody with a man you would do anything to get that same man and it just not for you, because sooner or later the same man gone because he never loves you anyway. That why I like people with a strong personality that can stand up and be a man or a women say no or yes and don't go back on your word even if it put them in trouble. So many time some of these inmate when they go before the judge from start to finish they say I never commit the crime even when they are under oat and cross examine to the end they still say I never do it., that apart of honoring god character to the end when the women lie on joseph to the end joseph say I never touch that women but they still put him away but he run with truth, so run with truth even when under pressure there are lot of hurting people in this world but be a restorer to help them for year I was hurt by some of the people close to me but I learn to forgive them and move on with my life god gave me. And continue to honor God big time move on and forgive who hurt you do Jesus say if you don't forgive who hurt you I God will not forgive you too your prayer and declarations and honor he will not hear and answer, so forgive and release it to God and move on all my reader obey Jesus and live.

Make ourself step up to God Jesus and please him in all way I see people do a lot to please family, friend and coworker go the extra mile nothing wrong with that, but make sure we go the extra mile for Jesus tell him in our action like go in the ocean, go in the valley, go in the prison and jail and preach for him spent quality time with Jesus some time days, whole week, whole month we talking step up to the plate of Jesus. Sometime you have to leave you family, job to do it be uncomfortable sometime for Jesus, he will restore you fully. I met a lady in Miami she was in prison but was release early for good behavior she tells me there was lady she met in prison she was there because she steal and give her husband, she in prison and the husband is free out here that going the extra mile for the wrong reason. Abraham story rock this man leave all his possession and heed it was just god voice he hear he never see good but he pack up and go step up to the plate of god because he want to give you a turnaround blessing but sometime you have to do what he want you to do, I see in the spirit people getting a turnaround blessing you shame shall be gone, I see in the spirit you getting a new name and new character, I see your whole family getting bless, I see world peace and prosperity and salvation people turning around to Jesus, I see children can play anywhere without be hurt, finally I see Jesus arrival is soon make sure you are ready, pray for the morning flight so we are ready to meet Jesus. That the prophetic word Jesus and the spirit gave me for you all receive it in your heart and believe expect it will happen when it happens call this ministry 754 368 9454 or call 1 888 731 1000 tell them apostle Claudia give you this word so we know it come to pass we want to hear.

I end this chapter with a prayer: "thank Jesus, you give us the special holy spirt to talk to you we can come boldly and talk face to face with you like Moses on mount Sinai, thank for caring and loving us the way you do, I pray that every born-again believer will receive the gift that makes us effective and well get the benefit of the special holy spirit in our personal life., amen

Apostle john was enjoying seeing the last day prophesy because he was in the spirit of God, he sees the new Jerusalem coming down from God prepare for all those who are ready and the voice of Jesus say to john "tabernacle of God is with men and we will dwell in that paradise and then we will come face to face with Jesus, God and the heavenly host but it under condition we have to ready to meet Jesus and enjoy all he has for us all. John gets advance in the spirit the angels carry john on pedestal stone like a high mountain and show him the beautiful city we all will inherit with diamond, gold and silver and peace, love and joy unlimited to enjoy no more war and pain. All nation African, European, which have Jesus mark in there heart and or save will enjoy it does matter our position it will be glory and honor Jesus spoke to john saying ":behold I come quickly blesses is he that kept the saying of the prophesy of this book and write it in their heart will be welcome and behold I Jesus come quickly and my reward is with me to give every man according as his work shall be I am the alpha and omega the beginning and the end the first and the last, I Jesus have send mine angels to testify unto you these things in all the churches I am the offspring of David and the bright and morning star" that Jesus word to spirit fill john I giving out there all the reason to have the holy spirit and Jesus will speak to you too just like john because he no respecter of person. The spirit and the bridge say "come and let him that heareth say come if you are thirst come and drink of this holy spirit water it given freely. So, we all that are children and apostle, pastors, evangelist, prophets, singing and members will tell someone the good news of Jesus is peace, is coming and is love so they can come to this spiritual feast be not ashamed of Jesus be bold as lion armless as dove which represent the holy spirit when Jesus just baptize the dove sat on his shoulder this is end of time prophesy get this word written in your heart and meditate on it day and night and most importantly do it. Jesus says "surely I come quickly"

I finish this book by saying it was a privilege to obey Jesus and write this book start writing it was 2019 thank Jesus in 2020 I could be able to finish it thank you Jesus. Thank my ever pressing publish miss Haley and the team she would call me always saying "Claudia is full time you finish this book people really need this encourage in this time of virus, and so much hurricane, tornado and disaster thank God I finally finish in Jesus precious name everything in your hand, and I trust you Jesus as my lord and savior, provider, healer and sustainer.

Call for prayer and donation: apostle Claudia Henderson ministry at 754 368 9454 or you can call trinity broadcasting network 1 888 8731 1000 we always looking for voluntary to witness Jesus' work, pray for people and help us with the feed of the homeless we are here for you amen and amen thank you Jesus.

BIBLICAL WORD AND MEANING

Abraham - Patriarch and father of us all that believe in Jesus

Canto - One who sing

Chumash - five books of Moses Jewish torah

Days of Awe - ten days from feast of trumpets to the day of atonement Gasol - Large or great

Hadassah – Jewish name for Esther the Queen

Israel - Name given to Jacob that later identified the sons of Jacob and was given to the land where they live

Keva - A fixed time fix words or prayer

Lucco - Tables or tablets refer to the ten commandments

Adam - mankind

Aaron - exalted one

Benjamin - son of the right hand

Boaz - Swiftness

David - Beloved, warrior and winner of all, God main Man

Elijah - My God is God

Elisha - My God is salvation go to heaven alive

Enoch - Dedicated to God and full of the Holy Spirit was translated to Heaven alive

Ephraim - Fruitful

Ezekiel - God Strengthens

Gabriel - God is my strength

Gideon - Feller of hewer

Isaac - laughter

Isaiah - God is salvation

Michael - who is like God

Jacob - Holder of the Heel

Jeremiah - the weeping prophet God uplift him

Joseph - He God will add

Matthew - Gift of God

Nathan - Gift giver

Noah - Rest comfort preacher of righteousness

Obadiah - Servant of God

Philemon - Affectionate Love

Reuben - Behold a son

Samuel - God has heard and Jesus is hearing all your prayer out there

Simeon - He God heard

Solomon - Peace, love and Joy with wisdom and understanding

Stephen - Crown and Jesus given you all the crown of salvation and beauty Day of Atonement - meaning sin forgiven

Buy these Book Pastor T, D. Jakes God turn pressure into Power, Breaking the Jewish code by Perry stone, Joyce Meyer unshaken trust, Andrew Warnock the Holy Spirit, Jordon Ruben Patient Heal thyself, John Grey Win within, Taaffe Dollar metal submission, Joel Osteen Living your Best Live now, John Hagee God 2-minute warning, Pastor Creflo Dollar the Holy Spirit your financial Adviser. Susan Heller the Holy Spirit the dumas Power.

Most important Book of all these Book even my book is the "HOLY BIBLE" and read it every single day. Thank for all your prayer and support because of "JESUS" and you people and faithfully fans we could preach, travel so you are special to us and God., you will get my next original book soon when Jesus gives it to me. THANK YOU ALL!